God's Plan,
Your Breakthrough

God's Plan, Your Breakthrough

Finding Purpose and Building
Resilient Faith Through Your
Darkest Moments

Simon Rockwell

JLS Publishers LLC

God's Plan, Your Breakthrough: Finding Purpose and Building Resilient Faith Through Your Darkest Moments
First Edition

Published by JLS Publishers, LLC
Spring Branch, Texas, USA
www.jlspublishers.com

ISBNs:
Paperback: 979-8-9988940-1-5
Hardback: 979-8-9988940-4-6
eBook: 979-8-9988940-7-7

Printed in the United States of America
First edition published in 2025

DEDICATION

To the broken, the burdened, and the brave. This book is for you.

To those walking through valleys no one else sees, who still whisper prayers in the dark and choose faith over fear, your courage humbles me.

To my wife, children, and faith community, thank you for being the steady hands that held me up when my own strength gave out.

Your love has been a lighthouse on my stormiest nights.

And to Jesus Christ, the author and perfecter of our faith, may every word in this book point back to Your grace, Your purpose, and the breakthroughs only You can bring.

Psalm 34:18

The Lord is close to the brokenhearted.

ACKNOWLEDGMENTS

This book exists because of the people who saw possibility in my brokenness.

To Stefaniya, my wife: You looked at a twice-divorced man carrying decades of guilt and somehow saw someone worth loving. Your faith saved me when I had none left. Спасибі, моя любов.

To our children: You show me every day that God's grace hides in scraped knees and bedtime prayers. Daddy isn't perfect, but Daddy's God is.

To my mother: You survived your own devastating losses and taught me resilience long before I knew I'd need it. Your strength after that crash near Fredericksburg gave me permission to believe the unsurvivable could be survived.

To my father: Our story wasn't simple, but I see you with clearer eyes now. The older I get, the more I understand the weight you carried and the choices you made. Thank you for the strength you passed down and for the pieces of yourself you never knew you were giving. This book carries your fingerprints too.

To Natalya: That introduction at the Hong Kong church changed everything. When I was ready to give up on love, you knew better.

To the Slavic community in Hong Kong: You embraced an American who couldn't speak your language but desperately needed your fellowship. You taught me that family isn't always blood.

To the JLS Publishers team, and to everyone whose story appears in these pages with names changed but impact eternal: thank you.

Most importantly, to Jesus Christ, who met me in a Caribbean police station, a Hong Kong ramen shop, and a thousand other broken places. Your grace is sufficient, even for someone like me.

To the family affected by that night in 1994: I think about you more than you'll ever know. I hope you've found peace.

Some names and identifying details have been changed to protect privacy.

AUTHOR'S NOTE ON STORYTELLING AND PRIVACY

The stories in this book were born out of real lives, real pain, and real grace. Some details, names, locations, timelines, and identifying elements have been adapted or blended to honor the privacy of the people who trusted me with their truth. Not every story appears exactly as it happened, yet each one reflects something real, something someone, somewhere, has lived or is living right now.

I wrote these pages with a single intention: to point beyond my failures, my healing, and my voice, and toward the faithfulness of God and the Lord Jesus Christ in every broken place. If any part of this book resonates with your own story, I pray it draws you closer to His presence, His mercy, and His unfailing love.

"For You have searched me, Lord, and You know me."

(Psalm 139:1)

May these pages remind you that nothing in your life is hidden from the God who sees every detail, holds every moment, and walks every valley with you.

Author's Note on Sacred Names: Throughout this book, I use the familiar English names "God" and "Jesus" for accessibility, but I want to honor their Hebrew origins that carry deeper meaning.

For Jesus: His Hebrew name is Yeshua (ישוע), a shortened form of Yehoshua (יהושע), meaning "YHWH saves" or "The Lord is salvation." When you read "Jesus" in these pages, remember you're reading about Yeshua—the One who saves.

For God: I primarily use "God" and "Lord," but these represent the rich Hebrew names that reveal His character:

- YHWH (יהוה) — The sacred Tetragrammaton, God's personal covenant name, often rendered as "LORD" in English Bibles

- Adonai (אֲדֹנָי) — "Lord" or "Master," expressing His sovereignty

- Elohim (אֱלֹהִים) — The Creator God, used in Genesis 1:1

- El Shaddai (אֵל שַׁדַּי) — God Almighty, the All-Sufficient One

When I write about the "Caribbean accident where God met me," know that it was El Roi (אֵל רָאִי)—"The God Who Sees"—who witnessed my darkest moment. When I describe finding grace, it's from YHWH Rapha (יהוה רָפָא)—"The Lord Who Heals."

Wherever you encounter "God" or "Lord" in this book, let your heart hear the fullness of these names—each one a facet of His character, each one a promise that He is enough for whatever you're facing at 4:47 AM or any other moment when the weight feels unbearable.

Even Gordon the Gecko knows there's something sacred in a name.

TABLE OF CONTENTS

PREFACE

Why This Book Exists

Right now, as I'm typing this at 4:47 AM on a Tuesday morning in October 2024, my coffee's already cold, and there's a gecko on my garage wall that's been staring at me for ten minutes. I named him Gordon. Gordon the Gecko watches me write about the worst night of my life, and somehow that feels appropriate. Even the lizards are witnesses to our breakdowns.

Let me back up.

In 1994, a fatal accident changed my life forever.

Not on purpose. But when you're behind the wheel, and someone dies, the "why" matters less than the weight. That weight? It's been sitting on my chest for thirty years now. Some mornings it's lighter. Some mornings, I can barely breathe. This morning, with Gordon watching and my kids still asleep, it feels like something in between.

You picked up this book for a reason. Maybe your marriage just imploded, and you're sleeping on your brother's couch, scrolling through your ex's Instagram at 2 AM. Maybe you just got the diagnosis, and the words "Stage 3" keep bouncing around your skull like a pinball. Maybe you're successful by every metric that matters to LinkedIn, but you're drinking vodka from a coffee mug during Zoom calls, and nobody knows.

I see you. Gordon sees you. God sees you.

Three weeks ago, I was at Costco buying entirely too much peanut butter (Stefaniya says six jars is excessive, but have you seen the prices lately?) when a woman recognized me from a men's breakfast where I'd shared the Caribbean story. She grabbed my arm by the rotisserie chickens and whispered, "My son just caused an accident. Someone died. He won't leave his room. What do I tell him?"

What do you tell someone whose world just shattered? You don't tell them it gets better. You tell them it gets different. You tell them the weight never fully leaves, but you get stronger carrying it. You tell them that grace shows up in the strangest places, like Hong Kong ramen shops and Texas Walmart's and yes, even Costco rotisserie chicken sections.

This book isn't a success story. It's a survival story. There's a difference, and if you don't know that difference yet, you will by the last page.

Look, my name is Simon Rockwell. I've made and lost fortunes. Been married three times. The first fortune? Tech stocks in '99. Had this company with "cyber" in the name (I know, I know), went from $400K to basically nothing while I was still in meetings pitching like everything was fine. I remember sitting in my car in the Wells Fargo parking lot off Westheimer, staring at that ATM receipt: $1,247.83. Three months earlier, I'd been a millionaire on paper. The receipt's still in my wallet. Don't know why I keep it. Maybe as a reminder that numbers lie.

The second fortune got eaten by divorce lawyers and bad Hong Kong real estate. Yes, you can lose money in Hong Kong real estate. Takes talent, but I managed it.

After that Caribbean night in '94, after the police station, after flying home with someone's death on my conscience, I went back to my hotel room and sat in the shower fully clothed for two hours. The water ran cold after thirty minutes. Didn't move. The cleaning lady knocked three times. I told her to go away in a voice I didn't recognize. Sounded like gravel in a blender.

I still think about him—often. The police told me not to contact the family. Said it would make things worse. But thirty years later, I still think about his family and pray for them. Right after, I check on Gordon.

Here's what I've learned: God's plan rarely looks like the blueprint we draw for ourselves. When I was ten, during an episode of "Lifestyles of the Rich and Famous," I sketched my dream house. Three stories. Wine cellar. Pool. Even calculated how being a lawyer would pay for it all. This kid from La Porte, Texas, whose mom fought hepatitis while pregnant with him, who came out at 4.5 pounds looking like an angry raisin with hair? That kid had it ALL figured out.

Found that notebook in 2013 when Mom sent me a care package to Hong Kong. The pages smell like mothballs and broken dreams now. I'd written "MY LIFE PLAN" at the top in red marker:

- Age 25: Graduate from law school

- Age 28: Make partner (didn't even know what that meant)

- Age 30: Marry someone who looks like Cindy Crawford

- Age 35: Buy my dream house

- Age 40: Have everything figured out

I'm 53 now. The only thing I got right was getting married by 30, and I screwed that up so badly I had to do it three times before God said, "Okay, Simon, let me just handle this one," and sent me Stefaniya.

The first time I saw her, I spilled borscht on my shirt. Not a drop. The whole bowl. Purple-red beet soup everywhere, looked like I'd been shot by a vegetable. She laughed and said something in Ukrainian to her friend Natalya. Found out later, she said, "At least he's not trying to impress me." That's when I knew she was different. Every other woman I'd dated, I'd performed for. Stefaniya got the disaster version from day one.

Let me tell you about Maria, because her story matters. Met her in a Kroger parking lot in 2019. I'd just backed into her car, barely a scratch, but I was having a bad day, and she was having a worse life. She got out, looked at the bumper, looked at me in my ridiculous midlife crisis BMW, and just started laughing. Not happy laughing. The kind that happens when crying takes too much energy.

"You know what?" she said. "I have cancer, three kids, and my ex just married his 22-year-old assistant. Your car can hit mine every day if it wants. I literally don't have the capacity to care."

We ended up sitting on that curb by the cart return for an hour. She told me how she'd found faith not in church (couldn't afford the gas), but in parking lot prayers between dropping kids off and chemo appointments. Her story is in Chapter 5, though I changed her name. She's beaten cancer twice now. Still texts me dad jokes that are so bad they're good. Last week: "Why don't scientists trust atoms? Because they make up everything!" I laughed alone in my garage for five minutes.

The stories in this book aren't fairy tales. Sarah's cancer journey doesn't end with magical healing. John's business failure doesn't get reversed by prayer. But what they build from the ashes? That changes lives. That's the real miracle. Not the rescue from the fire, but who you become walking through it.

Yesterday, I tried to create a spreadsheet for our family devotion times. Color-coded by kid. Metrics for "spiritual growth." Stefaniya took one look, grabbed my laptop, and said, "Simon, you cannot KPI your way into heaven. Also, you spelled Ephesians wrong." She's right. But I'm still the guy who thinks if I can just organize enough, control enough, plan enough, maybe the chaos will make sense. Spoiler alert: it doesn't.

Let me be crystal clear about something: This book isn't a substitute for professional help. If you're drowning in depression, anxiety, addiction, or having thoughts of self-harm, please reach out today. Call someone. Text someone. Walk into an ER if you have to.

For three years now, I've sat in a counselor's office twice a month. Dr. Patricia. She has this chair that squeaks when she leans forward to make a point, and she's made a lot of points about my "tendency to intellectualize trauma instead of feeling it." She taught me that faith and therapy aren't competing teams. They're dance partners. Some things need prayer. Some need Prozac. Some need both. There's no shame in any of it.

As I write this, my six-year-old Alex just burst into my office (the garage, let's be honest) to show me a drawing. Stick figures holding hands. Above us, he's drawn clouds with "GOD" written in backwards letters. Sometimes kids see clearer than adults who've logged a million airline miles searching for meaning.

Whether you're at the bottom of the stairs, halfway up and exhausted, or just trying to figure out which direction is up, this book is for you. Whether you're wrestling with your own life-changing moment or just feeling lost in the ordinary struggle of trying to keep everyone fed and nobody crying (including yourself), you're not alone.

Sometimes the most powerful breakthroughs come from simply learning to take the next step. Even when you can't see the top of the stairs. Even when you're not sure, there IS a top. Especially then.

So, let's climb together. One story, one prayer, one step closer to Him.

Because I've learned something in my 53 years of spectacular failures and unexpected grace: God's plan for your breakthrough probably looks nothing like what you've sketched out. And that's precisely why it will work.

Trust me on this. It's 5:23 AM now, the sun's starting to crack through those Texas oaks, and Gordon just caught a mosquito. Good for him. My coffee's gone cold again, but I'm still here. Still breathing. Still believing that somehow, God's using all this mess—the accident, the divorces, the failures, the therapy sessions, the ugly crying in my garage while the neighbors pretend not to notice—for something good. Not good like I planned it. Good, like He planned it.

And that's enough to keep climbing.

Welcome to the journey.

— Simon Rockwell, Texas, 2025

CHAPTER ONE

Faith in Motion

How God Uses Trials to Build Spiritual Strength

The prostate cancer scare hit different than the Caribbean accident.

With the accident, the crisis was immediate—blood, sirens, handcuffs, the whole catastrophic production. But sitting in my truck outside Texas Oncology & Hematology Center on a random Thursday in October 2025, waiting to find out if cancer was eating me from the inside out? That was slow-motion terror.

My PSA came back at 18.7. For context, normal is under 4. My buddy Mike was 12 when they caught him early. He's fine now, grilling on weekends, complaining about the Cowboys. Eduardo's brother hit 22. Dead in eight months. Left three kids and a mortgage.

I sat in that parking lot for forty-three minutes before going in. Counted every single one on my truck's dashboard clock. A woman parked next to me was sobbing into her steering wheel. We made eye contact for half a second. Both looked away. Both knew why the other was there. Some parking lots are just outdoor waiting rooms for bad news.

Dr. Ramirez (and yes, I thought of that Tex-Mex place on Highway 281 where Stefaniya and I had our third date) has this habit of clicking his pen exactly three times before delivering test results. Click. Click. Click. Like he's chambering rounds of reality.

"The biopsy shows inflammation, not cancer. Your levels are elevated due to chronic prostatitis. Treatable with antibiotics."

I started laughing. Not happy laughing. That unhinged kind that happens when your body doesn't know whether to celebrate or collapse. The nurse brought me water in a paper cup that said "Hope" on it. I kid you not. Sometimes God's irony is a little on the nose.

Driving home, I passed three churches. Baptist. Methodist. That new non-denominational one with the LED cross that looks like a nightclub logo. Didn't stop at any of them. Pulled into a Whataburger instead, ordered a honey butter chicken biscuit at 2 in the afternoon, and wrote "Thank You" on a napkin with a pen that was running out of ink. Left it on the dashboard like an altar offering.

That's faith in motion. Not the pretty kind you post on Instagram with sunset filters. The messy kind that happens in Whataburger parking lots with a mouth full of chicken and tears you pretend are from the jalapeños.

But this wasn't my first time learning that faith grows in the valley. Let me take you back to where it all started, to a phone call that changed everything.

That morning started like any other. Texas morning, kids still asleep, coffee half-made. The doctor's words were careful, clinical: "The test results are concerning. We need to discuss next steps."

Dr. Ramero, my urologist, had a name that made me think of a restaurant where Stefaniya and I once had a date. Strange, the places your mind goes when it doesn't want to face bad news. He always cleared his throat before delivering it, like a warning siren you could hear coming.

8

"Mr. Rockwell, your PSA levels came back at eighteen point seven."

I knew enough to know that was bad. Normal's under four. My buddy Mike from the men's group had gone through this last year; he was twelve, and they caught it early. Eduardo's brother wasn't so lucky. Twenty-two. Stage four. Dead in eight months.

The kitchen counter was cold under my palms. I could hear my neighbor's sprinkler system kick on, 7 AM like clockwork, even during the water restrictions. Guy waters his St. Augustine grass like it's the Sistine Chapel ceiling. Through the window, I watched a cardinal land on our fence, the one I keep meaning to fix where the pickets are loose. That bird shows up every morning, same spot, like he's checking to make sure we're still here.

"How long have I had it?" I asked, though that's not really what I wanted to know. What I wanted to know was: How long do I have left? Will I see our children graduate from high school? Will I walk my daughter Olivia down the aisle? Will Stefaniya have to do this alone?

"We need to do a biopsy first," my doctor said. "Can you come in on Thursday?"

Thursday. Three days away. Three days of knowing but not knowing. Three days of looking at my kids and wondering if I'm already a ghost.

Suddenly, I was 24 again, standing on a Caribbean roadside, watching paramedics work on a man whose name would appear on every legal document for the next two years. Time collapses when a crisis hits. Thirty years disappeared in an instant. I was back there, the weight of someone else's last breath heavy in the sticky island air. Tourists landing at the nearby airport, heading to paradise. Me, stranded in something else entirely.

The smell hit me first, that memory smell that trauma burns into your brain. Night-blooming jasmine mixing with the metallic tang of blood on hot asphalt, sweet flowers, and copper under the Caribbean humidity. The rental SUV's hood was crumpled just enough to trigger the insurance claim, but not sufficient to explain a death.

Of course, I know his name. You can't go through police reports, insurance claims, and legal proceedings without learning it. Saw it printed in the local paper. Heard it spoken in court. But I won't write it here. His family doesn't need to stumble across their loss in someone else's redemption story. He was 42. That's all I know. A fact from paperwork that tells you nothing about the man.

That's the thing about causing someone's death. You carry their absence without ever knowing their presence. Thirty years later, I still see those legal documents sometimes when I close my eyes. A whole life reduced to a case number. A name I'll never speak but can't forget.

Back on the roadside, the paramedic, a kid named Marcus with a scar through his left eyebrow, kept looking at me like I might collapse. "You hurt, mon?" he kept asking in that Caribbean accent that usually sounds musical, but that night sounded like a funeral hymn.

I wasn't hurt. Not physically. But something inside me broke that night, something that thirty years later still hasn't fully healed.

You'd think after carrying that weight for three decades, after two divorces and countless geographic escapes, I'd have figured out how to handle bad news. But there I was, gripping my coffee mug like it could anchor me to the present, realizing that faith isn't about avoiding storms. It's about knowing who's on the boat with you.

The doctor kept talking, discussing treatment options, success rates, and percentages that blur together when your mind is busy with different calculations. The arithmetic of loss. The algebra of what if. The calculus of prayers that feel like they're bouncing off the ceiling.

"Radical prostatectomy has an 85% success rate when caught at this stage," the doctor was saying. I heard "15% failure rate."

"Radiation therapy is less invasive but..." I heard "but you might die anyway."

"We have excellent outcomes with robotic surgery..." I heard "robot cutting into your body while you pray, it doesn't nick something important."

My phone buzzed. Text from Alex's school: "Reminder: Science fair project due Monday!"

Life doesn't stop for your crisis. It keeps demanding lunch money, homework help, and explanations for why the sky is blue, even when your sky is falling.

Your Faith Needs a Gym Membership

Here's the part nobody tells you about spiritual strength: it's not built in the moments of victory. It's built at 3 AM when you're arguing with God about why He allows suffering. It's built in hospital waiting rooms where the fluorescent lights make everyone look half-dead. It's built in the gap between what you thought your life would be and what it actually is.

I learned this from Tommy "Big Tom," we called him at the Miami men's group back in 2008. Six-foot-five, 280 pounds of former NFL prospect turned contractor. Guy could bench press a Volkswagen but cried like a baby when he talked about his wife, Sarah's, pancreatic cancer.

"Faith ain't muscle you flex at church," he told us one Thursday morning over questionable coffee at the Waffle House on Bird Road. "It's scar tissue. Gets stronger every time it heals from being torn."

Eight months later, I was a pallbearer at Sarah's funeral. We buried her on a Tuesday that hit 97 degrees with 90% humidity. South Florida heat trying to kill you even at funerals. Tom stood there in his black suit, the one she'd bought him for their daughter's wedding, sweating through the jacket but refusing to take it off. "She liked me in this suit," he said.

That's faith with its sleeves rolled up. Not pretty. Not Instagram-worthy. Just real.

Real strength isn't about being invincible. It's about learning to stand when you have every reason to fall. It's about discovering that sometimes the heaviest weights we lift aren't in any gym, they're the invisible burdens we carry every single day.

I learned this the hard way. After the accident in 1994, I thought that if I could move fast enough, accomplish enough, I could outrun the weight. I threw myself into business with the desperation of someone trying to earn back worthiness. Multi-million-dollar deals, international contracts, passport stamps collected like trophies. All of it was an elaborate attempt to prove to God, to the world, and to myself that I deserved to be here still when that man was not.

Want to know how desperate I was to keep moving? Singapore to Sydney for a four-hour meeting, then back the same day. Twenty-four hours in the air for four hours of talking about petroleum infrastructure that nobody would remember six months later. The airline flight attendant recognized me on the return flight. "Back already?" she asked. I lied about having another meeting. Truth was that stillness felt like drowning. Motion felt like swimming, even when I was doing laps in an empty pool.

The airline lounge became my second office. Had my own chair, back corner, and a view of the tarmac, close to the bar. The bartender, an elderly Chinese guy named Yìchén, knew my drink. Macallan 18, neat, with a side of self-loathing. Forty-seven dollars a glass. I did the math once and spent $11,000 on airport whiskey in 2010 alone. Ridiculous.

But here's what Paul knew that took me years to figure out: "Work out your salvation with fear and trembling" (Phil. 2:12). He wasn't talking about earning God's love through spiritual CrossFit. The Greek word he uses, "katergazomai," means to work something to completion, to carry it to its ultimate conclusion. He was talking about the daily reps of faith. The showing up when you don't feel it. The trusting when you can't see it. Believing when everything in your logical mind says it's foolish.

The Spiritual Weight Room Opens at 5 AM (Whether You're Ready or Not)

After the accident, I spent years running. Not physically, I kept showing up to work, kept climbing ladders, kept collecting achievements like indulgences that could buy my way out of guilt. I ran spiritually. Tried to outwork the guilt. Tried to out-achieve the shame. Built a career that spanned continents because staying still meant facing what I'd done.

My passport from those years looks like a manifesto of avoidance. Singapore: March 2009. Dubai: April 2009. Tokyo: May 2009. Sydney: Also, May 2009. Lagos: June 2009. Thirty-seven countries in eighteen months. I told people I was building an international consulting empire. I was really just building elaborate ways to exhaust myself into not thinking.

Each hotel room looked the same after a while. Same corporate art on the walls, abstract paintings that meant nothing to anybody. Same minibar prices that would make Jesus flip tables. Same CNN International playing the same fifteen-minute news cycle. The Marriott in Singapore had the same bedspread pattern as the Hilton in Frankfurt. Or maybe I just stopped noticing differences.

I remember sitting in a Hong Kong hotel room, probably my hundredth business trip, staring at the ceiling at 3 AM. The city lights outside created patterns on the walls, shadows, and illumination dancing together like my faith and doubt had been doing for years. The jet lag wasn't a problem. My soul was.

The hotel was one of those high-end resorts where the lobby smells like money and polished marble. I remember the numbers 28 and 40, because 28 was the age of my first panic attack, and 40 was the age I thought I'd finally have life figured out. Spoiler: I'm 53 now and still learning. The minibar had Johnnie Walker Blue at $127 for a two-ounce pour. More per ounce than the gold on my wrist. Didn't stop me from ordering three.

That night, the air conditioning hummed at a frequency that reminded me of the fluorescent lights in that Caribbean police station. You know how certain sounds can transport you? That hum took me straight back to 1994, to Officer Williams asking me to describe again what happened, to write it down, to sign my name to the worst night of my life.

That's when I picked up the hotel Bible, you know, those ones with the thin pages that feel like they might disintegrate if you breathe wrong. It fell open to Matthew 11:28: "Come to me, all you who are weary and burdened, and I will give you rest."

Rest? I didn't even know what that meant anymore. Rest felt like a luxury for people who hadn't taken lives. Rest was for people whose consciences didn't wake them at 3 AM with instant replays of the worst moment of their existence. Rest was for people who deserved it.

But that's the thing about grace, it doesn't check your deserving credentials at the door.

I sat there holding that Bible like it might bite me. The pages were so thin I could see my hand through them, like looking at an X-ray of faith. Someone had left a note tucked in the pages, written in pencil on the hotel stationery: "He loves you anyway. - Room 1128."

Room 1128. Someone else's crisis. Someone else's 3 AM wrestling match with God. And they'd left breadcrumbs for the next broken traveler.

In that moment, staring at those words, I stopped running for the first time in years. Not literally, I still had three more cities on the schedule that week. But spiritually, something shifted. I realized I had been trying to earn what was already freely given. Like a man dying of thirst beside a fountain, refusing to drink because he thought he had to pay for the water.

When Life Hands You Weights, Start Lifting

By the year 2000, I found myself getting baptized in the LDS church. Now, before my evangelical friends are tempted to close this book, stay with me. In my desperate search for structure and meaning, I threw myself into religious activity as if it were another business venture. Ward Mission Leader. Priesthood responsibilities. Teaching Sunday school. Leading missionary discussions. I was doing all the right things for all the wrong reasons, still trying to earn what had already been freely given through Christ alone.

The whole LDS thing started because of Elizabeth. Met her at a Ward singles dance near the temple in Orlando, February 2001. She had this laugh that made you want to be funnier than you were. Blonde hair, she was always tucking behind her ear when she was nervous. She explained the LDS faith like it was computer code, input righteousness, output blessings. For someone drowning in chaos, that structure felt like salvation.

The missionaries who taught me were Elder Patterson from Boise, a farm kid who'd never seen a skyscraper before his mission, and Elder Kim from Seoul, an engineering student who approached theology like calculus. They'd sit in my Miami apartment, sweating through their white shirts because I kept the AC at 78 to save money, teaching me about eternal families and celestial kingdoms.

"Why do you want to join?" Elder Kim asked during our fifth discussion.

"Because I need to be good enough," I said without thinking.

"Good enough for what?" Elder Patterson asked, genuinely confused.

"For God to forgive me for something."

They looked at each other, these two nineteen-year-olds who'd probably never gotten anything worse than a parking ticket.

"Brother Rockwell," Elder Patterson said slowly, like he was remembering something from training, "Christ's atonement already paid that price."

But I joined anyway. Got baptized in water heated to what felt like exactly 98.6 degrees; they have specifications for everything in the LDS church. Like God cares about water temperature.

See, I thought if I could just be religious enough, disciplined enough, obedient enough, maybe the weight would lift. Maybe the 3 AM replays would stop. Perhaps I'd finally feel forgiven. The LDS church, with its emphasis on worthiness and works, felt like a system I could master. Checkboxes I could tick. Levels I could achieve. It was faith as performance metrics, and I was determined to hit every KPI.

The thing about the LDS system is it's beautifully organized. Temple recommends interviews every two years, where they ask you specific questions. Are you morally clean? Do you pay a full tithe? Do you sustain the prophet? Fifteen questions total, I believe. I tried to memorize them. Practiced my answers in the mirror like I was preparing for a board presentation.

Bishop Smith, insurance salesman during the week, judge of worthiness on Sundays, would sit across from me in his office that smelled like old hymnals and Pledge furniture polish. He had this painting of Joseph Smith behind his desk, eyes that seemed to follow you. Made you feel guilty even when you hadn't done anything wrong. Recently, anyway.

"Brother Rockwell, do you have any sins that need confessing?"

Every. Single. Time. He asked like he knew something. Like God had sent him a memo about the accident. But I'd already confessed to three different bishops in three other wards across two states. They all said the same thing: it was an accident, not a sin. Move forward in faith.

However, moving forward and leaving behind are two distinct things.

I even baptized my own mother in April 2001. The water in that baptismal font was cooler than usual, and her tears were warm on my shoulder when she came up. She looked at me like I'd finally figured it out, like her broken son had finally found his way home. I wanted so badly for that to be true.

Mom drove up from La Porte in her 1995 Buick LeSabre, the one with the dented rear bumper from when she backed into a light pole at HEB. She brought a casserole, King Ranch Chicken, because "people need to eat after church." Even getting baptized into a new faith, she was still a Texas mother first.

The baptismal font was in a room that looked like a small swimming pool's corporate cousin. White tile, no windows, painting of the Jordan River on the wall. Mom wore this white jumpsuit that the church provided. Size medium, but she needed a small. It billowed around her like she was drowning in fabric.

"I'm proud of you, honey," she whispered when she came up from the water, mascara running despite the waterproof label.

I wanted to tell her not to be. That my reasons were all wrong: I believed I loved Elizabeth, but what I loved more was the structure I thought she and the LDS system could give me, scaffolding for a soul already collapsing. Only later did I learn that love without God's foundation can't hold. But Mom looked so happy. And I'd already caused her enough disappointment for one lifetime.

But here's what I learned: you can't systematize grace. You can't earn what's already free. You can't achieve your way to absolution.

The marriage that followed, built within that religious framework, was constructed on sand. We both were trying so hard to be perfect Latter-day Saints that we forgot to be human beings. We had Family Home Evening every Monday, attended the temple regularly, and fulfilled our callings faithfully. From the outside, we looked like the ideal LDS couple. Inside, we were drowning in expectations neither of us could meet.

Elizabeth and I lived in a subdivision outside of Miami. No two houses looked alike, with Mediterranean Revival villas next to Coastal Contemporary designs, and occasional Spanish Revival bungalows. Their brightly colored stucco exteriors stood in bold contrast to the lush, wilder landscaping of palm trees and tropical plants.

Our neighbor, Brother Mitchell, was in our ward. Used to check if our lights were on during Monday's Family Home Evening. "Just making sure you're keeping the commandments!" he'd say with this smile that never reached his eyes.

We'd sit in our living room with the curtains open so people could see us being righteous. Reading from the Book of Mormon while our marriage died one verse at a time. Elizabeth would make cookies, chocolate chip, always chocolate chip, and we'd eat them in silence, the only sound the ticking of the clock her mother gave us. A temple clock that chimed hymns on the hour. "Families Can Be Together Forever" at 8 PM. The irony wasn't lost on either of us.

The last Family Home Evening we had, neither of us spoke. Just sat there with our scriptures open, cookies uneaten, while that damn clock played "Love at Home." Two weeks later, she served me papers.

When it crumbled in 2007, I thought my faith would too. I'd done everything right according to the system. Paid my tithing. Kept the

Word of Wisdom. Wore my garments. Attended my meetings. How could God let it fail when I'd checked every box?

Instead, something strange happened. In the rubble of that marriage and that religious system, I found bedrock. Not the bedrock of an institution or a set of rules, but the bedrock of raw, desperate faith in a God who loved me not because of what I did but despite what I'd done.

C.S. Lewis wrote in *The Problem of Pain:* "God whispers to us in our pleasures, speaks in our conscience, but shouts in our pain: it is His megaphone to rouse a deaf world" (Lewis, 1940/2001). Brother, was He shouting. And for the first time in years, I was actually listening.

The Reps Nobody Sees

You want to know where genuine faith gets built? Not in the Sunday service with the worship band and the polished sermon. Not in the Bible study where everyone nods along to familiar verses. Genuine faith gets built on Tuesday afternoon when you're white-knuckling the steering wheel, trying not to fall apart. It gets built on Thursday night when you're on your knees because you've run out of clever solutions. It gets built in the spaces between what you proclaim on Sunday and what you're living on Wednesday.

I call it Tuesday Faith. Sunday Faith is easy, you're surrounded by people singing the same songs, saying the same "amens," wearing the same forced smiles. Tuesday Faith is when your kid gets suspended from school, your check engine light comes on, and your ex-wife texts about needing more child support, all within the same hour.

Thursday, February 22, 2007. My first marriage was officially over. The paperwork was signed, but what stung more was the silence that followed, the sudden absence of someone who had once been my whole world. That same week, my biggest client pulled out of the contract, and I felt the ground shift beneath me.

That was the season when Thursday's faith got tested, when the only prayer I could manage was 'Help' whispered into the bathroom mirror, wondering who I was supposed to be now.

By 2012, I was in Hong Kong, living apart from Josephine, my second wife. The marriage was unraveling, and though she had two daughters I loved as my own, the distance between us had grown into something I couldn't bridge. In a city of millions, I felt utterly alone. That's when faith stopped being a theory and became survival.

Let me paint you a picture: My apartment was 600 square feet of minimalist depression. White walls. IKEA furniture. A mattress on the floor because I couldn't commit to buying a real bed, which felt too permanent, too much like admitting I was actually living this life. The only color came from the convenience store beer cans accumulating on my counter, markers of nights spent arguing with God about why He kept letting me fail.

7-Eleven beer. Always Asahi. HK$10 per can. I kept them lined up like soldiers on the counter, an aluminum army of my failures. Seventeen cans by the window. I counted one night. That's HK$170 worth of trying not to feel. The lady at 7-Eleven, Amy (English name, probably not her real one), started giving me this look. Not judgment. Worse. Pity.

"You okay, sir?" she asked once at 11:47 PM when I was buying my usual three cans.

"Yeah, just hot tonight," I lied. It was March and maybe 65 degrees.

She threw in a free pack of tissues. "In case," she said in English so broken it was almost impossible to understand. But I understood.

21

She'd seen enough expats crying into convenience store beer to know the signs.

I'd walk the streets of Hong Kong at night, past the salarymen stumbling out of bars, past the love hotels with their discreet entrances, past the 24-hour convenience stores glowing like chapels of capitalism. I was carrying my broken faith like a backpack full of rocks. Some nights I'd end up at this little ramen shop in Causeway Bay. Eight seats. One chef. No English menu.

The owner didn't speak English. I didn't speak Mandarin Chinese beyond "xièxie" and "bù hǎoyìsi." But somehow, over steaming bowls of noodles, I felt less alone. There was something sacred about that silent companionship. He'd nod when I walked in, prepare my usual order without asking, and occasionally push a free side of gyoza across the counter with a look that said, "I don't know what you're carrying, but eat this anyway."

Mr. Chen. That was his name. Found out after six months when his daughter came to help one night. University student, perfect English, studying finance at HKU.

"My father says you're very sad," she said matter-of-factly while refilling my water glass.

"How does he know? We don't speak the same language."

"Sadness needs no translation," she said. "He says you remind him of himself after his wife died. Same eyes. Like you're looking for someone who's not coming back."

That's where God met me. Not in some grand cathedral. Not in a moment of spiritual epiphany. In an eight-seat ramen shop, 8,000 miles from home, where the only prayer I could manage was the wordless

22

gratitude for hot food and human kindness.

Your Workout Partner Shows Up in Unexpected Ways

March 2015. Hong Kong. For three years, I'd been trying to break into the Slavic community there. You haven't experienced feeling like an outsider until you've been the only American in a room full of Russians, Ukrainians, and Kazakhs, all speaking languages that sound like poetry and machinery had a baby.

My first Slavic church service was like walking into someone else's family reunion, where everyone forgot to tell you the dress code. The women wore headscarves. The men wore suits that looked like they'd survived the Soviet Union. I showed up in khakis and a polo like I was going golfing.

The babushka in the front row turned around, looked me up and down, and said something in Russian that made everyone within earshot laugh. Found out later, she said, "Americans dress like they're always on vacation."

My friend Natalya from Russia finally took pity on me. We met at some international business mixer, one of those awful networking events where everyone pretends to care about your business card while looking over your shoulder for someone more important. But Natalya was different. She actually listened when I talked. She laughed at my terrible attempts at Russian pronunciation. She invited me to her church.

Natalya worked for a logistics company, helping Russian businesses navigate Hong Kong's banking system. She had this way of tilting her head when she was really listening, like a bird trying to understand human speech. Her English was perfect, but she'd sometimes drop articles, "We go to church" instead of "We go to the church" in that endearing way that reminded you she was translating constantly in her head.

"There's someone you should meet," she said one day over coffee in Tsim Sha Tsui. "Ukrainian girl. Just came back from Thailand. I think you two would... understand each other."

"Natalya, I'm 43, twice divorced, and carrying enough baggage to fill a cargo plane."

"Perfect," she said. "She likes projects."

I almost didn't go to that gathering. What was the point? Two failed marriages. A faith that felt more like scar tissue, tough, numb, barely alive. I was 43 years old, living in a country where I couldn't even read most of the street signs, carrying guilt from something that happened before some of the people in that room were even born.

But something, call it God, call it desperation, call it the fact that I had nothing better to do on a Saturday night, made me show up.

I wore my best suit. The humidity had other plans. By the time I got to the church, I looked like I'd been swimming fully clothed. My hair was doing that thing where it gives up and just lies flat against your skull in defeat. I was about to leave when Natalya grabbed my arm.

"You look terrible," she said cheerfully. "Perfect. Now she cannot think you are trying to impress."

Stefaniya walked in, and I swear the room shifted. Not in some romance novel way. More like when you're doing bench press and someone adds weight you didn't expect. Suddenly, everything required more effort. Breathing. Thinking. Not saying something monumentally stupid.

She was wearing this simple black dress and had her hair pulled back in a way that showed she'd rushed there from somewhere else. Later, I learned she'd been teaching English to kindergarteners all day, five-year-olds who'd worn her out but somehow hadn't dimmed the light in her captivating gray eyes.

First thing she said to me: "You're the American who keeps coming to our church but doesn't understand anything."

"That's me."

"Why do you keep coming?"

"I don't know. Maybe I'm hoping understanding will suddenly kick in."

She laughed. Not a polite laugh. A real one. "Like divine Google Translate?"

"Something like that."

Within weeks, I was telling her things I'd never told anyone. About the accident, not the sanitized version I'd crafted for public consumption, but the real one, with all the blood and guilt and 3 AM terrors. About the failures. About the nights I wondered if God had made a mistake letting me live when that man died. She listened, not the polite listening where someone's waiting for their turn to talk. Real listening. The kind that makes you feel less alone in your story.

You know what she said when I finally told her everything? She didn't say "It wasn't your fault" (though legally it wasn't). She didn't say "God has a plan" (though He does). She said, "So God's not finished with you yet."

That floored me. Not "You're broken." Not "You need therapy" (though I did). Just an acknowledgment that I was still under construction.

We married that December at the Hong Kong city courthouse. No big ceremony. No fancy reception. Just two broken people deciding to let God write a redemption story with the pieces.

The ceremony was at 2:30 PM on December 18, 2015. The courthouse smelled like industrial cleaner and had broken dreams; half the people there were getting divorced. We were the only ones smiling. Viktor, this giant Russian guy from church, was my witness. Kept wiping his eyes and claiming it was allergies. In December. In Hong Kong.

Stefaniya wore a simple white dress she'd bought the day before at H&M. Sixty dollars. She looked like a million bucks. I wore the same suit I'd sweated through when we first met. Seemed appropriate, starting how we began, imperfect but real.

The justice of the peace was this elderly Chinese woman who'd probably married thousands of couples. She looked at us, this middle-aged American with baggage and this young Ukrainian woman with hope, and said, "You two have old souls. This will work."

The Training Never Stops (And That's the Point)

Last week's garage prayer session was interrupted by Alex at 5:47 AM. He's carrying his sister's doll, one of those American Girl knockoffs from Target that costs $30 instead of $130. Head completely detached, arm bent the wrong way, dress torn.

"Daddy, can you fix this?"

I'm looking at this disaster of a doll, thinking about everything I've tried to fix. Marriages, zero for two. My relationship with my dad is still in progress. My guilt, thirty years and counting. Some things stayed broken despite my best efforts. Some things got worse when I tried to fix them.

"I can try," I told him.

The superglue was in the kitchen junk drawer, that graveyard of good intentions. Dead batteries, expired coupons, instruction manuals for appliances we don't even own anymore. I pulled out the hardened tube and thought about how often I've tried to patch my life together with quick fixes that never really hold. God doesn't use superglue. He rebuilds from the inside out, stronger than before, making what's broken whole again.

As I'm working on reattaching this doll's head with superglue and prayers that it holds, Alex asks, "Daddy, why do things break?"

How do you explain entropy to a six-year-old? How do you tell him that everything tends toward chaos, that breaking is easier than building, that sometimes things break and stay broken?

"Because we live in a world where breaking happens," I said. "But that's why we learn to fix things. And when we can't fix them, we learn to make something new with the pieces."

He thought about it. "Like Legos?"

"Exactly like Legos."

He watched me work for a moment, then said, "Maybe breaking isn't so bad if you can make something new."

Out of the mouths of babes.

That's really what this whole faith journey has been: learning to make something new with broken pieces. The accident broke my sense of safety and control. The divorces broke my understanding of commitment. The denominational journey broke my neat categories for God.

But here's the thing about broken pieces: they fit together in ways that whole things never could. They create patterns that perfect pieces could never make. They let light through in places that were solid before.

YOUR NEXT STEP

This week, identify one weight you've been trying to carry alone. Write it down in detail, not the sanitized version, but the real one with all its jagged edges. Then share it with one safe person. Could be a counselor. Could be a pastor. Could be a friend who's earned the right to hear your story.

Remember: God's gym doesn't require perfect form, just showing up. And the strongest people aren't the ones who never fell, they're the ones who learned to get back up.

The weight might feel too heavy. Good. That's how you know it's working.

CHAPTER TWO

Stories That Strengthen

Why Testimonies Fuel Courage and Connection

The fluorescent lights in the Caribbean police station hummed at a frequency that matched my panic. Twenty-four years old, sitting on a metal chair that conducted the air conditioning straight through my bones, creating a physical cold that matched the spiritual freeze happening in my soul. My hands wouldn't stop shaking, not from the temperature, but from the knowledge settling into my body like sediment in still water: someone was dead, and I was behind the wheel.

The chair had this crack in the plastic seat, right where your tailbone hits. Every time I shifted, which was every ten seconds because anxiety makes you fidget, it pinched. I focused on that pinch like it was the only real thing in a world that had suddenly gone surreal. The police station smelled wrong. Not criminal wrong, but Caribbean wrong. Pine-Sol mixed with salt air and that sweet rot smell that tropical flowers get when they're dying. There was a poster on the wall about drunk driving, half in English, half in what I think was French Creole. Shows a car wrapped around a palm tree. I hadn't been drinking. Stone cold sober. Sometimes God doesn't need alcohol to let lives collide.

Detective Sergeant Williams, whose brass nameplate was tarnished around the edges, had been on the force for seventeen years. He told me that while we waited for his partner. Said it like he was proud of it, like lasting seventeen years in paradise was an accomplishment. Maybe

29

it was. His wedding ring caught the light every time he wrote something down. I kept thinking about his wife at home, probably used to late-night calls, probably used to him coming home with other people's tragedies stuck to his uniform like cigarette smoke.

The detective across from me had kind eyes, which somehow made it worse. He spoke with that island lilt that usually sounds like music, but that night it sounded like a funeral dirge.

"Mr. Rockwell, I need you to tell me again what happened. Take your time."

"Take your time." Like time was something I had. That was when the other officer came in, speaking rapid Creole. He wasn't talking to me, but to Williams. He didn't know I'd studied French in college— enough to catch fragments. Words drifted across the room: mama... hospital... children... They hung there like ghosts, pieces of a story I wasn't meant to hear.

I wanted to unhear them. Wanted to go back five minutes when the victim was just 'the deceased,' not a real person with a real life I'd ended. The officer mentioned something about him being known in town, a regular at the local bars. Dark clothing, walking outside the crosswalk, probably impaired. But none of those facts changed what I'd done.

Take my time. As if time hadn't just stopped for someone. As if a family wasn't about to receive the worst phone call of their lives. As if my entire understanding of myself as a good person hadn't just shattered like a windshield on impact.

Outside, the island continued its evening routine with cruel normalcy. Reggae music drifted from a bar down the street, Bob Marley singing about three little birds, every little thing being alright. Tourists laughed over rum punches, their vacation continuing while my life cleaved into before and after. Life went on, except for one man whose name I didn't yet know, whose family I'd never meet, whose story had just ended where mine took its darkest turn.

A couple walked past the station window. She wore a white sundress that glowed under the streetlight like she was made of moonlight. He had his arm around her waist, protective, possessive, in love. They were probably walking back from dinner at one of those beachfront restaurants where they serve fish you watched them catch that morning. Normal people having a typical night, fifty feet from where I sat, trying to explain how I'd ended someone's everything.

I wanted to bang on the window. Wanted to scream at them to pay attention. To look both ways. To understand that any second, any random Thursday night at 9:47 PM, your whole life can pivot on someone else's footstep in the wrong place at the wrong time.

When Everything You Believe Gets Tested

I'll be honest with you. Growing up in La Porte, Texas, getting baptized at our local Episcopal church when I was 51 days old, my mother insisted on doing it early because I'd been born so premature she was afraid of losing me, none of that prepared me for that night. We'd gone to Sunday school in that little church with the red doors and the stained glass that turned morning light into rainbows. I'd learned about David and Goliath, Daniel in the lion's den, and Jonah in the big fish. Stories where faith always won, where God always showed up in time, where the good guys walked away unscathed.

Mrs. Henderson ran our Sunday school with an iron fist wrapped in a velvet glove. She smelled like White Shoulders perfume and always had butterscotch candies in her purse, the kind in the yellow cellophane that crinkled so loud during prayer time that everyone knew you were sneaking candy. She had this felt board where Bible stories played out in fuzzy, sanitized scenes.

David was always this confident kid with perfect aim. No mention of him later sending Uriah to die so he could steal his wife. Daniel in the lion's den looked peaceful, like he was at a petting zoo. No talk about survivor's guilt, about why God saved him but not his friends. Jonah's whale looked like it was smiling. Nobody explained what three days in fish stomach acid would actually do to human skin. Or that Jonah was depressed and suicidal after Nineveh repented, angry at God for showing mercy.

We sang "Jesus Loves Me" every single week. Simple. Clean. Four-four time. "Yes, Jesus loves me, the Bible tells me so." But what happens when you're not sure Jesus loves someone who just killed someone's father? But what happens when you're not sure Jesus loves someone who just killed somebody's son or father? What happens when "the Bible tells me so" isn't enough to wash blood off your conscience, even when the blood was legally not your fault?

Nobody taught me about the believers who didn't get delivered. Nobody mentioned the apostles who were martyred, the faithful who suffered without relief, the prayers that seemed to bounce off heaven's floor. Nobody prepared me for sitting in a police station, trying to explain to a God I thought I knew why He'd let this happen before my eyes.

Sitting there, I tried to pray but couldn't find God in the formal words I'd learned. The Lord's Prayer felt like a foreign language. The 23rd Psalm, "though I walk through the valley of the shadow of death," felt like mockery. So, I just bled honestly: "I don't know how to carry this. I don't know how to be someone who caused this. I don't even know if You're listening to someone like me anymore."

What actually came out was less coherent. More like: "God... I... why didn't You... I can't... please..." Fragment prayers. Broken words. The kind of prayer that's just hemorrhaging in God's general direction, hoping He's got gauze.

Detective Williams gave me a plastic cup of water. The kind you get at dentist's offices, so small it's almost insulting. Like my thirst for absolution could be quenched with two ounces of warm tap water that tasted like pipes.

"You religious, Mr. Rockwell?" he asked while we waited for paperwork.

"I was this morning," I said without thinking.

He nodded like that made perfect sense. "Lot of people find God in this room. Lot of people lose Him here too."

The part no one ever admits about spiritual crisis is how quiet it is. No thunderbolts. No voice from heaven. No dramatic music to mark the revelation. Just you and the weight of what you've done, sitting under harsh lights that make everything look guilty, wondering if the Jesus you learned about in Sunday school, the one who said, "Come unto me, all ye who are heavy laden," could possibly care about someone who just took a life, even if it was an accident.

The First Testimony That Saved Me

Three weeks after returning from the Caribbean, I was sitting in a Denny's on Westheimer at 2 AM. Near the Galleria in Houston. One of those 24-hour beacons for insomniacs, shift workers, and the

33

functionally destroyed. I'd been there every night for a week, in the same booth, back corner, where the red vinyl was cracked, with a view of both the exit and the parking lot. You develop habits when you can't sleep. Rituals that make you feel like you have some control over something.

The waitress, a woman named Dolores with silver hair and glasses on a chain, kept refilling my coffee without asking. She wore those white orthopedic shoes that nurses favor, the ones that squeak on linoleum like they're announcing your arrival to the afterlife. Her uniform had a coffee stain shaped like Florida on the pocket. She smelled like maple syrup and Virginia Slims, that particular perfume of someone who's seen enough life to know it's gonna kill you anyway, might as well have some pancakes and a smoke while you wait.

Fourth cup, she sat down across from me.

"Honey, I don't know what you're carrying, but I recognize the look. I wore it for ten years after my son died."

I looked up, really looked at her for the first time. The lines around her eyes weren't just from age; they were topographical maps of grief.

She pulled a photograph from her apron pocket without me asking. Worn soft at the edges from handling. A boy in a baby-blue tuxedo, the kind from the '80s with the ruffled shirt, stood next to a girl in a pink catastrophe of taffeta and hope.

"Daniel," she said his name like a prayer. "May 15, 1987. Seventeen years old. Hit an oak tree on Dairy Ashford coming home from prom. His date, Jessica, was in the passenger seat. Broke her pelvis in three places, but she lived."

Dolores traced her son's face in the photo with one finger, gently, as if she could still feel him through the Kodak paper.

"June 1988, Jessica showed up at my door. Ninety pounds if she were wearing boots. Her mama drove her, waited in the car with the engine running like they might need to make a quick escape. This child stood on my porch apologizing for surviving. For walking when Daniel couldn't. For graduating when he didn't. For having a future he'd never see."

Dolores poured more coffee even though my cup was still full. The ritual mattered more than the result.

"You know what I told her?" She set the pot down and looked straight at me. Really looked at me. "I told her that survivor's guilt is just love with nowhere to go. It's not a sin. It's not a weakness. It's proof that you recognize the weight of life. But honey, you can't carry someone else's death forever. At some point, you must let God carry it for you."

She patted my hand and went back to her shift. I never saw her again. Switched to a different Denny's because I couldn't handle the kindness. But her words stuck. Love with nowhere to go. That's what guilt felt like. Care and concern and sorrow for someone I'd never known but whose absence I'd caused.

Brother Martinez and the Ministry of Shared Scars

Years later, after I'd joined the LDS church, thinking structure would save me, after that marriage fell apart and I'd moved to a different congregation, I met Brother Martinez. Former gang member from East LA, tattooed hands that he'd hid under long sleeves at church, eyes that had seen too much but somehow still held light.

The first time I saw Brother Martinez, I thought he was security. Six-two, maybe 250 pounds of what looked like previous bad decisions turned into current muscle. Shaved head that reflected the chapel lights. Goatee trimmed with mathematical precision. He stood by the door greeting people, and when he shook your hand, you felt the calluses of someone who'd worked with more than prayers.

"Welcome, brother," he said. His voice was softer than his appearance suggested, like thunder trying to whisper.

He always wore long sleeves, even in Miami's August hell. I found out why three months later. His arms were a manuscript of his former life. "XIII" on one forearm, his gang. A skull with a crown on his bicep. The Virgin of Guadalupe on his shoulder, only beautiful thing in a gallery of regret.

The first time I heard his testimony, I nearly walked out of the chapel. He was talking about his past, about a night in 1987 when he'd killed a rival gang member. The details were different, intention versus accident, gun versus car, but the weight was the same. That haunted look when he talked about the victim's mother at the trial. The way his voice cracked when he mentioned seeing the man's children in the courtroom.

"Ricardo," he said the name clearly, like he was calling roll in heaven. "Nineteen years old. Liked to draw cartoon characters. His mama brought his sketchbook to the trial. Page after page of superheroes he'd invented. One was called 'Peacekeeper.' Had the power to stop bullets."

The congregation went silent. You could hear the air conditioning struggling, the kid in the mother's room crying, someone's stomach growling. Real life continuing while we sat with the weight of ended life.

"I threw up," Martinez continued. "Right there in the courtroom.

On the defense table. My lawyer's briefcase. The bailiff had to get maintenance. The judge called a recess. Ricardo's mother was named Teresa. She walked over while they were cleaning. I thought she was going to spit on me. Curse me. Something. She handed me a tissue and said, "You look like my Ricardo when he was sick."

I was already halfway to the door when he said something that stopped me: "I know some of you are thinking you could never relate to a former gang banger. But I guarantee there's someone in this room who knows what it's like to be responsible for ending a life. And brother, sister, whoever you are, you're not alone, and you're not unredeemable."

He found me in the parking lot after service. Didn't say anything at first, just stood next to me while I pretended to check my phone. Finally: "I see it in your eyes, Hermano. That look that says you've taken a life."

"I didn't mean to," I said. First words I'd spoken to another human who might understand.

"Neither did I," he said. "I mean, I meant to shoot. Meant to scare. Maybe meant to wound. But I didn't mean for him to die. Didn't mean for him to bleed out on Whittier Boulevard while his girlfriend screamed. Didn't mean to become someone who'd killed someone. But meaning and doing, they're different countries, hermano."

We sat in his truck for three hours: a 1985 Chevy C-10, primer gray with rust eating the wheel wells. The bench seat had duct tape patches like battlefield surgery. A rosary hung from the rearview mirror next to a faded air freshener that had given up. The whole cab smelled like WD-40, Old Spice, and redemption.

He told me about the night in detail, the confrontation, the gun that seemed to fire itself, the kid (because that's what they both were, kids) bleeding out on Whittier Boulevard while sirens wailed in the distance. About the fifteen years in Chino, most of it in solitary because former gang members don't last long in general population. About the day a prison chaplain introduced him to a Christ who was executed as a criminal and understood what it meant to die condemned.

"You know what the worst part was?" he said, looking through his windshield at the empty church parking lot. "It wasn't the guilt. It was believing I was beyond forgiveness. I could accept that God might forgive me; He's God, forgiveness is His thing. But I couldn't forgive myself. Took me ten years to realize I was making myself more important than God. If He says I'm forgiven, who am I to disagree?"

He reached into his glove compartment and pulled out a book, The Return of the Prodigal Son by Henri Nouwen. Dog-eared, notes in every margin, coffee stains on the cover. "This Dutch priest gets it," he said. "Read it when you can't pray. And Hermano? You call me when the weight gets too heavy. Day or night."

He wrote his number on the inside cover: 305-555-0198. "That's my cell. I keep it on vibrate during service, but I keep it on."

I still have that book. Page 47 has a coffee ring where I set my mug down while crying too hard to keep reading. Page 92 has a tear stain that warped the paper. Page 144 has blood on it from a nosebleed I got during a panic attack. The book looks like what it is, evidence of a wrestling match with grace.

The more I traveled for work, and I traveled constantly, as if motion could equal progress, as if geographical distance from the Caribbean could somehow translate to emotional distance. The more I found these stories. Not always in churches. More often in hotel bars at 2 AM, when jet lag and whiskey loosened tongues. In airport lounges during weather delays, when strangers became temporary confessors. In late-night conversations with people who would never see me again, which somehow made the truth easier to tell.

Singapore Airlines lounge, Changi Airport, December 2008. My flight to Sydney was delayed six hours. I was on my third Tiger beer, they're free in the lounge, which is dangerous for someone trying to numb themselves on a corporate expense account.

This British guy in a wrinkled Savile Row suit sits down next to me. His eyes were red-rimmed in that way that could be exhaustion or could be crying in an airport bathroom. I knew that look. I'd worn it.

"You ever lose someone?" he asked without preamble. No "hello." No "is this seat taken." Just straight to the existential crisis. That's how you know someone's drowning: they skip the small talk.

"Yeah," I said, not specifying whether I meant "lost" as in death or "lost" as in caused death.

"My daughter. Sophie. Nine years old. Leukemia."

The way he said it, like he was reading items off a grocery list. Factual. Flat. The tone you use when emotion would split you in half.

James ordered a Tiger. Then another. By the fourth one, he was telling me about Sophie's stuffed rabbit, Mr. Hoppy, that she'd had since birth. How she insisted they put him through the MRI machine first so he wouldn't be scared. How the oncology nurses played along, gave Mr. Hoppy his own hospital bracelet. How they buried Mr. Hoppy with her because, his voice cracked here, "she might need him wherever she's going."

I'll be the first to admit, I know alcohol isn't ideal for a Christian.

39

Never been my proudest habit. But it's something I've wrestled with, something I'm still working on. And in those years, it was often the glass in my hand that opened doors to conversations I never would have had otherwise. Broken people recognize broken people. Sometimes it takes a beer to admit it.

"I cursed God for two years straight," James said, his accent getting thicker with each drink. "Not metaphorically. I mean, I would stand in my garden in Kent at 6 AM every morning, before my wife Margaret woke up, and literally curse at the sky. Used words that would make a sailor blush. Told God exactly what I thought of His plan, His wisdom, His bloody mysterious ways."

He gestured with his bottle like he was conducting an orchestra of rage. "Sophie's swing set is still in that garden. Can't bring myself to take it down. I'd stand there and tell God exactly what kind of bastard He was. Helped me get through breakfast without crying into my corn flakes."

"What changed?" I asked.

"Nothing dramatic. Few months ago, I was in Singapore on business. Wandered into a chapel in Chinatown, probably just escaping the heat. A woman stood up to share about losing her son. Chinese, maybe sixty. Her English was broken, but her pain was fluent. She said something I'll never forget: 'I was so angry at God for taking my boy. Then I realized God knows what it's like to watch His Son die. He's the only one who really understands.'"

James stared at his beer. "Started me thinking differently. Faith isn't about understanding, mate. It's about still showing up when understanding fails."

We sat there until they announced our flight, his to London, mine to Sydney. Six hours of drinking and talking about dead children and absent Gods. When we finally stood to leave, he swayed a bit and caught himself on my shoulder.

"You know what Sophie said near the end?" His breath was sour with beer and grief. "She said, 'Daddy, I think God must be very sad to need so many angels.' Nine years old, and she was trying to comfort me about her own death."

I never saw James again. But I think about Sophie's theology sometimes. Maybe God is sad. Maybe that's why He seems so quiet sometimes, too heartbroken to speak. A Father who knows exactly what it costs to lose a child, sitting with us in our rage, waiting for us to realize He's the only one who really understands.

Jerusalem and the Palestinian Shopkeeper

Easter Sunday, 2005. I was standing at the Western Wall in Jerusalem, surrounded by thousands of pilgrims, each carrying their own stories of faith and doubt. I had gone to Jerusalem on business, a technology conference that happened to coincide with Holy Week. I told myself it was a coincidence. Looking back, I see God's fingerprints all over it.

The conference was at the International Convention Center. "InnoTech 2005: Bridging Digital Divides." A bunch of tech executives pretending we were changing the world while really just trying to sell more software. I'd extended my stay through Easter; told my boss it was for "relationship building." Really, I needed to stand where Jesus stood. Needed to see if holy ground could make me feel less like damaged goods.

The Western Wall was smaller than I'd imagined. You see pictures and expect this massive monument to faith. But it's human-sized. Touchable. The stones worn smooth by millions of hands, polished by the oil of desperate palms pressing prayers into rock.

I watched an elderly woman next to the mechitza, tears streaming down her weathered face as she pressed a folded paper into a crack between ancient stones. Her lips moved in silent prayer, which could have been Hebrew, Arabic, or Aramaic for all I knew. But I recognized the desperation in the posture. The way she leaned into the wall like it might hold her up. The way her fingers lingered on the stone was as if she was reluctant to break contact with something holy.

My own prayer, written on International Convention Center stationery (the irony wasn't lost on me): "God, I killed someone (by accident). Can You still use me?" Folded seven times until it was small enough to wedge into a crack that probably held a thousand similar questions.

The man next to me, expensive suit, Swiss watch, looked like he ran a hedge fund, was sobbing. Forehead pressed against the wall, shoulders shaking. A folded paper fell from his pocket when he pulled back from the wall. I glimpsed the words before he snatched it up: 'Let her live.' Three words. Whole world in them.

Later, walking the Via Dolorosa, the path tradition says Jesus walked to the crucifixion, I stopped in a small shop to escape the crowds and the heat. The owner, a Palestinian Christian named Yusuf, served me Arabic coffee in a cup no bigger than a shot glass. The coffee was thick, bitter, cardamom-scented, and somehow exactly what I needed.

The shop was maybe ten feet by twelve feet. Shelves crammed with olive wood crosses, ceramic tiles with Bible verses, bottles of Jordan River water that looked suspiciously like tap water. Tourist faith for sale. But in the back corner, Yusuf had a small table with two chairs, a hot plate with an ibrik for making coffee, and a photo that changed everything.

"You look troubled, friend," he said in accented English. "Jerusalem does that, brings out what we carry inside."

Perhaps it was the ancient city, maybe the coffee, maybe the fact that I was 7,000 miles from anyone who knew me, but I found myself telling this stranger about the accident. Not the sanitized version I'd crafted for public consumption, but the real one, the sound of impact, the way time slowed down, the weight of knowing someone's last breath happened because of me.

Yusuf listened without interrupting, refilling my tiny cup twice. When I finished, he pulled out a photograph from under his register. A young man in a Barcelona soccer jersey, frozen in mid-kick, pure joy on his face.

"My son. Amir. Sixteen years old. Best footballer in East Jerusalem." His voice carried pride and pain in equal measure. "Second intifada. Wrong corner, wrong moment. The soldier who shot him was also sixteen."

He poured more coffee, the ritual giving us both something to do with the silence.

"March 15, 2002. 3:47 PM. He was walking home from practice. The soldier thought his soccer ball was something else. By the time he realized..." Yusuf shrugged, a gesture that contained all the pointlessness of young men dying over misunderstandings.

"For one year, I planned revenge. Made lists of names and addresses, studied their patrol patterns. My wife stopped speaking to me. My daughter stopped singing; she has a voice like an angel, but after Amir died, she has no more songs. You know what revenge gave me? Diabetes from the stress. Insomnia. A heart so full of hate there was no room for anything else."

"What changed?"

"I read Matthew 18. Peter asks Jesus about forgiveness. How many times? Seven? Jesus says seventy times seven. I realized I was drinking poison, waiting for others to die. So, I chose to stop drinking poison. I chose to pour coffee instead."

That's when I noticed it behind his register, next to Amir's photo: a small Israeli flag and a Palestinian flag, crossed like friends' arms.

"The soldier came here two years ago. Just showed up one day, no uniform, shaking like a leaf. We drank coffee. We cried. He told me he sees Amir's face every night. I told him so, do I. Now he comes every month. We remember Amir together. Is this not better than revenge?"

"His name is David," Yusuf continued. "Good Jewish boy from Tel Aviv. Studies computer science now. Wants to make apps that connect Palestinians and Israelis. Every month, on the fifteenth, he comes. We drink coffee. We look at pictures of Amir. Sometimes we cry. Sometimes we laugh, and I tell him stories of Amir's pranks. David brings his mother sometimes. She makes this cake, babka. We eat cake and remember our boys, the one dead, the one who might as well be, for how much he's changed."

I bought an olive wood cross I didn't need. Yusuf wrapped it in newspaper, and I saw the date, April 2, 2005. Six days after Easter. Eleven years after my accident. Time moves different when you're counting from tragedy.

The Digital Church That Saved My Faith

Fast forward to 2014. I'm in Rio de Janeiro, Brazil, for a petroleum conference. The Copacabana Palace Hotel's Wi-Fi crashed during a million-dollar video conference call. In my frustration, I stormed out to find an internet café, cursing in three languages, when I heard laughter coming from a corner table.

The café was called "Cyber Beach," which should have been my first warning. Luminous lights that belonged in an interrogation room. Computers from 2003 running Windows XP. The air conditioning was broken, and the place smelled like burned coffee and digital desperation. But in the corner, at a laptop held together with duct tape, was this woman, just radiating joy.

Maria, maybe forty years old with eyes that sparkled despite apparent exhaustion, was running an online Bible study from her laptop. The screen showed faces from everywhere: a grandmother in Caracas, Venezuela, sharing one phone with five others; someone logging in from rural China at what must have been 3 AM their time; a family in a Colombian refugee camp, with children sleeping on the floor behind them.

"Miren, amigos," Maria was saying in Spanish, then switching to English, then Portuguese. "Look at Psalm 137. 'How can we sing the Lord's song in a strange land?' This is our question today, yes? How do we worship when we're far from home?"

Her setup was incredible in its simplicity. A webcam that looked like it came from a cereal box. A microphone held together with electrical tape. The laptop's screen was cracked in the corner. But she had sticky notes everywhere, in three languages, with names and prayer requests. "Chen's mother, surgery Tuesday." "Ahmed, family reconciliation."

"Esperanza, husband missing 74 days."

Forty-three people were logged in. I know because I stood there counting, trying to understand what I was witnessing. This wasn't a church service. It was something more raw, more real. People were typing their prayers in the chat. Someone in Venezuela wrote: "No food for two days, but I have internet at the library, so I'm here." Someone else from Iran: "If they find me watching this, prison. But I need fellowship."

During the break, Maria noticed me hovering. "You want to join? Everyone is welcome."

She made me sit down, share her one headphone, the left speaker was broken, so I could hear better. Her breathing was labored, lungs working too hard for simple tasks. Found out later she had lupus. Her immune system attacking itself while she used her remaining strength to hold together believers across six continents.

I learned Maria had been a traditional missionary to Brazil until lupus grounded her. "For six months, I was so angry. I thought God benched me. I trained my whole life to serve, and then my body betrays me. But then I realized, Paul planted churches through letters. I just have better Wi-Fi."

She introduced me to her digital congregation, each name coming with a story that made my own pain feel both smaller and more connected to a larger tapestry of suffering:

"This is Esperanza. Her husband disappeared three months ago; the government took him. Still prays for his return every meeting."

"This is Ahmed. Muslim background believer. His family held a funeral for him when he converted. He's dead to them but alive in

Christ."

"This is Chen. She risks arrest every time she logs in. But she says the risk is worth it for the community."

When I complained about the hotel's internet destroying my business deal, Maria laughed, not mockingly, but with genuine joy. "Your business uses technology for profit. We use it for prophets. Which one changes lives forever?"

The conference call that brought me there? Lost the deal. Three million dollars, gone because of a Wi-Fi glitch. But sitting in that sweltering café, watching Maria shepherd believers across the globe with broken equipment and unbreakable faith, I realized I'd been measuring success wrong my whole life.

When Your Testimony Finds You

March 2015. Hong Kong. I'd been in Hong Kong for three years, working, existing, not really living. My second marriage ended with the kind of quiet devastation that doesn't make for dramatic stories but leaves you just as broken. No infidelity, no big betrayal, just two people who couldn't figure out how to build something together.

The divorce was final on a Thursday. I remember because Thursday was our taco night, and I was standing in ParknShop holding a packet of Old El Paso taco seasoning, $62 HKD for shells that were probably stale, when it hit me: I'd never make tacos in that apartment again. Josephine, her name still catches in my throat sometimes, had left a Post-it on the refrigerator: "Water the plant." That was the summary of our marriage. A dying spider plant and an instruction to keep it alive.

My friend Natalya from the Slavic Christian community kept insisting I meet this Ukrainian woman named Stefaniya. "She understands complicated journeys," Natalya said. That should have been my first clue that this would be different.

The introduction happened at a potluck after church. Russians take potlucks seriously. This wasn't your American church potluck with tuna casserole and Jell-O salad. This was borscht and pelmeni and holodets, which is meat jelly and sounds awful but is weirdly good, and approximately seventeen different versions of salad with mayonnaise.

Stefaniya brought kutia, this Ukrainian Christmas dish made with wheat, poppy seeds, and honey. Except it was March. When I asked about it, she said, "Christmas food for non-Christmas days. Sometimes you need a celebration when there's nothing to celebrate."

Stefaniya's testimony floored me. Not because it was dramatic, no accidents, no crimes, no massive conversions. But because it was faithful. Raised Christian Orthodox in Ukraine, moved to Hong Kong alone for work, chose faith over cultural convenience when it would have been easier to just blend in. She talked about trust like someone who'd actually practiced it, not theorized about it.

Three months into our relationship, sitting in a tiny restaurant in Mong Kok, I told her everything. About the accident, every detail, including the ones I usually edited out. About the sound that still woke me at night. About the guilt that felt like a physical weight on my chest. About how I'd spent twenty years trying to earn my way back to worthiness.

We were at this hole-in-the-wall place called Happy Kitchen, an ironic name for where I was emotionally vomiting my worst trauma. Ten tables crammed into a space meant for five. The couple next to us was close enough that I could read their text messages. But somehow, in that cramped space with strangers' elbows in our personal space, I felt safe enough to tell the whole truth.

I waited for her to make excuses to leave. To suddenly remember an appointment. To do that thing people do when they realize they're sitting across from someone more broken than they signed up for.

Instead, she reached across the table and took my hand. "Simon, God doesn't waste our pain. He redeems it. Your story isn't finished. This terrible chapter? It's not the ending. It's the part where God starts writing the redemption."

Her English wasn't perfect, she said "wasted" like "vest-ed" and sometimes dropped articles. But her theology was flawless. She understood redemption not as erasure but as transformation. Not pretending the bad never happened, but believing God could make something beautiful from the wreckage.

We got married that December. Just a simple courthouse ceremony in downtown Hong Kong. Viktor from the Orthodox church was my witness, and Natalya was hers. No fancy reception, just dinner at that same ramen shop in Causeway Bay where I'd spent so many nights wrestling with God over steaming bowls of noodles.

Mr. Chen, the ramen shop owner, gave us free gyoza. His daughter translated: "My father says happiness looks good on you. Less sad eyes." Even Mr. Chen had become part of my testimony, this Buddhist man who'd fed me through my darkest nights without knowing he was being used by a God he didn't believe in.

The Stories We Tell Ourselves

Here's what I've learned after 50-plus years of stumbling toward grace: testimonies aren't just for church. They're the stories we tell ourselves at 3 AM when doubt creeps in through the cracks in our faith.

49

They're the truth we cling to when life stops making sense and God feels distant as the stars.

My mother's testimony shaped me before I even knew I needed shaping. She told me about her first husband, John, and their baby dying in that crash outside Fredericksburg. Told it matter-of-factly while making chicken fried steak, grease popping in the cast iron skillet she'd inherited from her mother.

"The luggage flew forward," she said, turning the meat with a fork. "Crushed the baby on impact. John's neck snapped when we hit the ravine. Doctor said he didn't suffer. Like they'd know."

She let that sit there between us, heavy as the humidity before a storm.

"Sometimes God saves us from things," she'd say, usually while doing something mundane like washing dishes or folding laundry. "And sometimes He saves us through things. Both are salvation."

Brother Martinez's story gave me permission to believe God could use broken people, not just slightly dinged people who'd made minor mistakes, but genuinely broken people who'd done irreparable damage. His testimony taught me that redemption isn't about erasing the past but about God writing a new future despite it.

That Palestinian shopkeeper in Jerusalem showed me that forgiveness isn't a feeling but a daily choice, like choosing coffee over poison. Every morning, Yusuf makes that choice. Some mornings it's easier than others. But he makes it anyway.

Maria's digital church from that Rio de Janeiro café taught me that ministry happens wherever broken people gather to remind each other that God is still good, even when life isn't. Especially when life isn't.

And Stefaniya? Her testimony is still being written, intertwined with mine now, teaching our three children that faith isn't about perfection but about presence. About showing up even when you're scared, broken, confused. About trusting that God is still writing, even when you can't read the handwriting.

YOUR NEXT STEP

This week, share one honest truth about your struggle with someone you trust. Not the polished version meant for public comfort, but the real one—the unfinished, uncomfortable one that makes you wonder whether God could still work through you.

Here's what often happens next: they open up too. That's how testimony works. Vulnerability invites vulnerability. When you show your scars, others feel safe to reveal theirs. Suddenly, you're not alone—you're surrounded by people God is rebuilding, one broken piece at a time.

Your story may become someone else's lifeline—the thing they cling to when they feel like they're sinking. Don't soften it. Don't dress it up. Just tell it honestly and trust God to use it as He sees fit.

Your hardest moment may be the very thing that allows hope to pass through you. God doesn't erase brokenness; He redeems it. And the cracks in your story? That's where the light gets in—and where it shines out for others.

CHAPTER THREE

Pain with Purpose

Why God Allows Suffering And What It Builds in Us

I still remember the smell of jet fuel mixing with plumeria that night in the Caribbean in mid-1994. Sweet flowers and industrial fumes, paradise and machinery colliding in my nostrils just like life and death had collided on that highway. The rental SUV's keys felt heavier than they should have in my pocket as I stood there on the main island road, watching paramedics work on a man I'd never met but whose face I'd never forget. Dark clothing against dark asphalt. Outside the crosswalk. Those details replay like a broken record, even thirty years later.

The rental was a red SUV from the local car rental company. Cost me forty-seven dollars a day plus insurance, which I'd nearly skipped, thank God I didn't. The irony of thanking God for insurance while someone lay dying because of me wasn't lost, even then. I'd picked it up three days earlier, joking with the counter girl about how these things flip easier than pancakes. She'd laughed and said tourists always wanted something flashier, but ended up settling for whatever was left. "At least it has air conditioning," she'd said, her island accent turning it into music.

The impact wasn't loud. Movies prepare you for crashes to sound like explosions. This was more like dropping a bag of wet cement. A thud that had finality to it. No echo. Just done.

The man, I wouldn't know who he was for another three hours, was wearing a short-sleeve work shirt, light cotton, sweat-darkened at the collar. The fabric looked like it had seen a hundred hot days on the job. One of his hiking boots had been torn off in the impact. It lay nearly twenty feet away, laces still tied, as if the force itself had pulled him straight out of it.

The paramedics moved with practiced efficiency, but I could read the truth in their body language. The way they slowed down after the initial rush. The subtle shift from urgency to protocol. One of them looked at me, a young guy, probably not much older than I was, and I saw recognition in his eyes. Not of me personally, but of the situation. He'd seen this before. Driver meets pedestrian. Physics wins. Life loses.

His name tag said "Marcus." Had a small scar through his left eyebrow that made him look perpetually skeptical. When he walked over to check on me—standard protocol to make sure the driver wasn't having a heart attack—his boots made a sucking sound on the asphalt. The road was still wet from the afternoon rain that comes every day at 4 PM in the Caribbean, like God set a timer.

"You hurt, mon?" he asked, shining a penlight in my eyes.

I wasn't hurt. Not on the outside. But something inside me gave way that night, with the same finality as the man's last breath. Thirty years, three marriages, and more new addresses than I can count haven't patched the crack it left.

You want to know what wrestling with God really looks like? It's not some poetic struggle in a prayer closet with soft lighting and background music. It's standing on the side of a Caribbean road at 9:47 PM (I'll never forget the time), watching someone's last moments while tourists drive by rubbernecking, and trying to understand how a business trip turned into someone's last day on earth. It's spending the next eighteen hours at a police station that smells like mildew and instant coffee, signing statements in triplicate. It's flying back to Texas with that weight in your chest, knowing you're going home, but someone else isn't, ever.

Two days later, I was on Flight 1247 bound for Dallas via Miami to meet another client. Middle seat because I'd booked it last-minute after the police finally released me. The woman next to me was reading a Danielle Steel novel. The guy in the aisle was snoring before we left the gate. And I sat there, still wearing the same polo shirt that had his blood on the sleeve, just a few drops I didn't notice until the plane's bathroom mirror showed me, trying to understand how everyone could act so normal when the world had fundamentally changed.

The Questions That Haunt

In those first months after, I couldn't look at my reflection without seeing a killer. That's the word that echoed in my head during those 3 AM wakeups when the ceiling became my confessor and the darkness my only companion. I'd trace the popcorn texture of my apartment ceiling with my eyes, following the same pattern night after night, like maybe if I traced it enough times, I'd find God's explanation hidden in the randomness.

My apartment in Houston's Montrose district, $625 a month for 750 square feet, which was a good deal even in 1994. The bedroom faced east, which meant sunrise came through the blinds like an interrogation light. I'd taken to taping aluminum foil over the windows, and I told people it was to keep the apartment cool. Really, I just couldn't stand the light. Light felt like judgment. Darkness felt honest.

The couple upstairs worked different shifts. She left at 5 AM for her hospital admin job. I could hear her heels clicking across their floor. He came home at 2 AM from bartending, constantly dropping his keys by the door, in the same spot every night. Their routine became my clock. Her heels meant I'd survived another night. His keys meant I had three more hours to wrestle with God before dawn.

"Why do You let good people die and guilty people live?"

That question became my nightly prayer, if you can call an accusation a prayer. I'd throw it at the ceiling, at the sky, at the God I'd grown up believing was both all-powerful and all-loving. The math didn't work. If He's omnipotent, He could have prevented it, made me leave the hotel thirty seconds later, made the man cross thirty seconds earlier, made the streetlight brighter, made something, anything, different. If He's all-loving, He would have prevented it. So, either God wasn't who I thought He was, or I was missing something fundamental about how He operates.

I did the math obsessively. If I'd left the restaurant thirty seconds later. If I'd stopped to tie my shoe. If I'd taken a different route. Thirty seconds. That's all. The length of a commercial. Half a stoplight. The time it takes to wash your hands properly (happy birthday sung twice, according to my mother).

The victim would be alive for thirty seconds.

The silence that answered me was deafening. But somewhere in that silence, after weeks of sleepless nights and days that blurred together like watercolors in rain, I started hearing something else. Not a voice, I want to be clear about that, because people always think God speaks in dramatic ways. More like a presence. Like when my mother used to sit on my bed when I was sick as a kid back in La Porte, not saying anything, just being there. Her weight on the mattress edge, creating a little valley that I'd roll toward. That's what God's presence felt like, a subtle weight in the room, creating a gravity that pulled me toward something I couldn't name.

The Lie We Tell About Faith and Suffering

Let me save you some disappointment right now. If you picked up this book thinking I'd tell you how to avoid pain through prayer, you grabbed the wrong one. If you want a testimony about how faith makes life easier, how following Jesus means smooth sailing, how enough belief equals enough protection, return this book now. Get your money back. Buy something else. It took me decades to learn that faith does not prevent suffering. It transforms it.

I learned this first from Mrs. Rodriguez at the elementary school in La Porte. Her son David was born with cerebral palsy. She'd bring him to school sometimes when his aide was sick. David, in his wheelchair that cost more than her teacher's monthly salary, typing on a communication board with one finger, each word a victory against muscles that wouldn't cooperate.

Some mom at a PTA meeting once said, "God never gives us more than we can handle." Mrs. Rodriguez looked her dead in the eye and said, "Then God must think I'm a lot stronger than I am, because I can't handle this. I just show up anyway."

David died when I was in fifth grade. Pneumonia. At his funeral, Mrs. Rodriguez didn't say any of those platitudes we throw around like confetti at tragedy. She said, "David suffered. I suffered watching him suffer. God suffered watching us both. That's the reality. The miracle isn't that suffering ends. The miracle is that love persists anyway."

I learned this while watching my parents' marriage fall apart when I was ten. I'd lie on the top bunk, crying into my pillow, listening to them fight downstairs about money and all the little things couples fight about when love slips into routine and routine slips into resentment. Their voices would carry up through the heating vents, muffled but unmistakable. Dad's low rumble of frustration. Mom's higher pitch of disappointment.

The worst fight was about a boat. Dad had bought a used bass boat without telling Mom. $3,200 that we didn't have. Mom found out when the check bounced, and the grocery store called. I can still hear her voice: "A boat, Robert? A BOAT? We can't afford milk that doesn't come from powder, and you bought a BOAT?"

Dad defended it as an investment. Take clients fishing. Business development. Mom threw a plate. It shattered against the kitchen wall; left a dent we painted over but never fixed. You could still see it if the light hits right—a scar in the sheetrock that matched the one in their marriage.

I'd pray the prayers kids pray: "God, please make them stop fighting. Please make them love each other again. I'll be good. I'll clean my room. I'll stop lying about brushing my teeth. I'll do anything."

But the fights continued. The marriage ended. And I learned my first lesson about suffering: sometimes it just happens, regardless of how hard you pray or how good you try to be.

Biblical Heroes Weren't Immune

You know what really irritates me? Sanitized Sunday School versions of biblical heroes. I remember sitting in that little Episcopal church in La Porte as a kid, watching flannel board presentations of Job smiling while losing everything. The teacher would move the felt pieces around, Job's sheep, gone. Job's camels, gone. Job's children, gone. And felt-Job just stood there with the same serene smile, like someone had told him his Netflix subscription had expired, not that his entire family had been killed.

Mrs. Patterson, our Sunday school teacher, had this way of making Bible stories sound like episodes of "Mister Rogers' Neighborhood." Everything was beautiful in God's neighborhood. She'd move those felt pieces around the board with her arthritic fingers, humming "Trust and Obey" under her breath.

"And Job never complained," she'd say, adjusting felt-Job's felt-smile. "He just trusted God."

Even at eight years old, I knew that was garbage. My goldfish died, and I cried for three days. Job lost ten kids, and he just smiled? Come on.

The real Job? He wanted to die. He cursed the day he was born. That's in chapter 3, folks. Look it up. The man literally said, "May the day of my birth perish, and the night that said, 'A boy is conceived!' That day, may it turn to darkness; may God above not care about it; may no light shine on it" (Job 3:3-4, NIV).

That's not patient suffering. That's a man in so much pain he wishes he'd never existed. That's a man who's lost ten children, not in some abstract theological exercise, but actual human beings he'd raised and loved and watched grow. Dead. All of them. In one day. And he sat in ashes, covered in boils that he scraped with broken pottery, and basically told God, "I wish You'd never made me."

I finally understood Job when I met Harold at the Dallas VA hospital in 2016. Harold lost three sons. Two in Iraq, 2004 and 2007.

One in Afghanistan, 2011. Different wars, same flag-draped coffins.

We were sitting in the world's most depressing cafeteria, luminous lights making the green Jell-O look radioactive. Harold was stirring his coffee with a plastic spoon that kept bending.

"People keep telling me about Job," Harold said. "Like that's supposed to help. You know what? [expletive] Job. At least his kids all died at once. I had to go through it three times. Three times watching my wife pick out caskets. Three times hearing 'Taps' played. Three times folding a flag into a triangle that's supposed to somehow represent a life."

Harold's honesty was more biblical than any flannel board could ever be.

That's honest faith. That's what it looks like when everything breaks and you're too exhausted to pretend it's okay.

But here's what grabbed me, what kept me reading Job during my worst nights. In the middle of his rant, while he's still oozing pus and grief, while his friends are telling him he must have sinned to deserve this, while his wife is telling him to curse God and die, Job says: "I know that my redeemer lives, and that in the end he will stand on the earth. And after my skin has been destroyed, yet in my flesh I will see God" (Job 19:25-26, NIV).

He said that with sores covering his body. With his children's graves still fresh. With friends accusing him of secret sin. That's not cleaned-up faith. That's faith with blood under its fingernails, dirt in its hair, and tears cutting tracks through the ashes on its face.

Paul's Thorn and Our Thorns

Paul's another one we've sanitized. When I was in Malta on business in 2011, I stood where tradition says Paul was shipwrecked. The Mediterranean was violent that day, waves crashing against the rocks with the kind of force that makes you understand how ships become splinters. I thought about him writing from actual dungeons, not metaphorical prisons, not spiritual challenges. Real chains. Real guards. Real rats. Real possibility of execution at any moment.

St. Paul's Bay in Malta is a tourist trap now. Fifteen euros for a beer. Twenty-five for fish and chips that taste like cardboard soaked in grease. But if you walk past the souvenir shops selling "I Got Shipwrecked in Malta" t-shirts, past the tour buses full of cruise passengers on a three-hour Biblical excursion, you get to the actual rocks.

Standing there, watching the Mediterranean try to destroy the coastline one wave at a time, I thought about Paul. Not apostle Paul. Not Saint Paul. Just Paul. A guy chained to a Roman guard, puking his guts out from seasickness, watching the boat that was supposed to take him to trial become driftwood.

Yet from those cells, he writes: "I have learned the secret of being content in any and every situation, whether well fed or hungry, whether living in plenty or in want" (Philippians 4:12, NIV).

What secret, Paul? Tell me. Because I'm drowning here, and contentment feels like a foreign language I'll never learn to speak.

I bought a replica Roman coin from a street vendor that day. Five euros for a fake piece of history. The vendor, an old guy missing his front teeth, said, "You know Paul was a prisoner here? Chains and everything. Still preached. Crazy man."

Crazy man. Maybe that's what faith looks like from the outside. Insanity. Finding joy in chains. Peace in storms. Purpose in pain.

The secret wasn't avoiding suffering. It was finding Christ in the middle of it. Not around it. Not over it. Through it.

Paul had what he called a "thorn in the flesh." Scholars have debated for centuries what it was, eye problems, epilepsy, chronic pain, persistent temptation. But here's what we know: he begged God three times to remove it. Three times. This is the apostle Paul, the guy who raised the dead, who survived shipwrecks and stonings, who saw the third heaven. And God said no.

"My grace is sufficient for you, for my power is made perfect in weakness" (2 Corinthians 12:9, NIV).

Not "I'll fix it." Not "It'll get better." Not "Here's why this is happening." Just "My grace is sufficient."

I've prayed that prayer, Paul's prayer, more times than I can count. "Take this away." The guilt. The memories. The 3 AM replays. The weight that sits on my chest like a stone. Take it away.

The answer's always the same. Not audible. Not dramatic. Just this quiet knowing that the thorn stays, but the grace increases. Like interest on an investment I didn't make, dividends on suffering I didn't choose.

Some days, that has to be enough. Some days, it's all we get.

The Framework That Actually Works

After years of spectacular failures, two divorces, a life-altering tragedy, and more geographic and denominational moves than a military family, I've developed what I call the Faithful Navigation

Framework. Not because I'm some guru. Because I've crashed enough times to recognize the patterns, like a pilot who's studied every black box recording, learning what makes planes fall from the sky.

I actually wrote this framework on a napkin first. Waffle House on I-45 North, somewhere between Houston and Dallas. 3 AM, because that's when all great theology happens, when you're too tired to intellectualize and too awake to ignore the truth. The waitress, Brenda, according to her name tag, which was held on with medical tape, kept refilling my coffee without asking. Seventh cup. At some point, caffeine stops being a stimulant and becomes a sacrament.

The napkin's still in my Bible, with a brown ring from where I set my coffee mug on it. Five steps written in ballpoint pen that skips, so some words are only half there. Like my faith most days, partially visible, requiring imagination to fill in the gaps.

Step 1: Acknowledge the Pain

Three months after that night in the Caribbean, I was sitting in a Denny's at 2 AM, pushing eggs around my plate like they were puzzle pieces that might reveal God's plan if I arranged them right. The waitress, probably in her 60s with that particular exhaustion that comes from too many night shifts and too many broken dreams, refilled my coffee and said, "Honey, whatever it is, pretending it ain't there won't make it go away."

Her name was Dolores; I know this because I became a regular at the Denny's on Westheimer. She had this way of knowing who needed to talk and who needed silence. For three months, I got silence and coffee. That night, apparently, I graduated to intervention.

"You've been coming here twelve nights in a row," she said, settling into the booth across from me with her own cup. "Same booth. Same order. Two eggs over easy, wheat toast, and hash browns. You eat maybe three bites. That's not hunger bringing you here."

She was right. It was the need to be around life at the deadest hour of night. To hear silverware clinking, proof that normal people were doing normal things while I sat there trying to understand how I'd become someone who'd ended someone.

I hadn't said a word to her about anything. She just knew. Maybe it was the way I was sitting. Maybe it was the untouched food. Maybe it was the look that every sufferer recognizes in another sufferer, that hollow-eyed stare of someone carrying invisible weight.

Jesus said, "Blessed are those who mourn, for they will be comforted" (Matthew 5:4, NIV). Not "blessed are those who stuff it down and soldier on." Not "blessed are those who put on a happy face." Blessed are those who mourn. Present tense. Active grieving.

When Mom finally told me about her first husband, John, and their baby dying in that crash outside Fredericksburg, I was forty-five when she shared the whole story; she didn't pretty it up. We were sitting at her kitchen table, the same one where she'd made me countless peanut butter sandwiches as a kid, where I'd done homework while she cooked dinner, where we'd had a thousand ordinary moments that suddenly felt sacred in light of what she was sharing.

The table was Formica, that indestructible 1960s kind with the metal trim. Aqua blue with gold specks, like someone had tried to make the ocean fancy. One corner was chipped, where Dad had dropped a wrench while trying to fix the ceiling fan at the table, because Mom said he was making a mess in the garage.

"The luggage in the back crushed the baby on impact," she said, her

64

voice steady but her hands shaking slightly as she held her coffee mug. Same mug she'd had since 1987 "World's Best Mom" in letters that had mostly worn off, so it read "W ld's B st M m." "John's neck snapped when we hit the bottom of the ravine. The doctor said he didn't suffer, but how would they know? How does anyone know what those last seconds feel like?"

She let me see her tears, fifty-three years after the fact. That's acknowledgment. That's refusing to let time diminish the weight of loss.

Step 2: Reflect on Scripture (But Really Wrestle)

Don't throw verses at pain like band-aids. Wrestle with them. Fight them. Argue with them. God can handle your honesty; He put Job, Ecclesiastes, and half the Psalms in the Bible, after all.

My Bible from those years looks like a crime scene. NIV Study Bible, the one with the navy-blue hardcover. Bought it at Mardel Christian Store for $47.99, thinking a new Bible would mean a new start. Within six months, it looked like I'd been performing surgery on it.

Coffee stains on Genesis through Deuteronomy, that's from the all-nighter trying to understand why God hardened Pharaoh's heart. Was free will real or not? Tear stains on Psalms, especially Psalm 22, "My God, my God, why have you forsaken me?" Jesus said that on the cross. If Jesus felt forsaken, what chance did I have?

My NIV Study Bible looks like a war zone. I am horrible with a coffee cup, as I have stains throughout my Bible. Tear stains on Romans 8. Margins full of arguments with God, questions, doubts, and occasionally, breakthroughs. Next to Psalm 88:13, I wrote in red ink: "REALLY?? This is supposed to help??"

Because Psalm 88 ends with darkness. No resolution. No happy ending. Just: "darkness is my closest friend" (Psalm 88:18, NIV). Sometimes that's where you are. And God included that in His Word for a reason because He knows that sometimes faith looks like sitting in darkness and still calling out to a God you can't see or feel.

I took that Bible to a men's retreat once. A guy named Chuck saw it during small group, all marked up and worn out. "Brother, you need a new Bible," he said.

"No," I told him. "I need this one. It's got my fight with God in it. You don't throw away the ring after a wrestling match just because it's got blood on it."

The Psalms saved my sanity. David was a train wreck who happened to write songs. "How long, LORD? Will you forget me forever? How long will you hide your face from me?" (Psalm 13:1, NIV). That's in the Bible. The man after God's own heart, asking if God has forgotten him. If someone that close to God can feel that distant from God, maybe my own distance doesn't disqualify me.

Step 3: Engage in Prayer (Even When It's Just Showing Up)

Prayer isn't performance. Sometimes it's just showing up, like going to a job you hate because you need the paycheck. Sometimes prayer is just breathing in God's direction.

In my Kowloon apartment, on the 27th floor, unit 2707, I remembered it because I was 27 when I first got married, and it ended in '06. The universe has a cruel way of joking. There was this spot by the window, just a square of floor where the morning sun broke through. Every day at 5 AM, I sat there with a cup of instant coffee from 7-Eleven, bitter enough to taste like regret.

Some mornings I prayed with words that almost sounded polished. Most mornings, I just stared at Lion Rock through the smog and asked a single word: "Help."

Anne Lamott says there are really only three prayers: "Help," "Thanks," and "Wow." During that season, I was stuck on "Help." Just "Help" on repeat, like a skipping record. Help me understand. Help me carry this. Help me believe You're still there. Help me want to keep living. Help.

I never met Anne Lamott, but her book *Help, Thanks, Wow: The Three Essential Prayers* (2012) reshaped my prayer life. She once said that sometimes the shortest prayers are the only ones that make it through the ceiling. That line stuck with me because it felt true, raw, simple, and enough.

Step 4: Find Community Support (This Is Non-Negotiable)

This might be the hardest step for guys like me who think we should handle everything solo, who were raised to believe that real men don't need help, that weakness is something to hide rather than share.

After my second divorce, I found a men's group that met at a hole-in-the-wall diner in Miami. Thursday mornings, 6 AM. Terrible coffee that tasted like cigarette ashes. Fluorescent lighting that made everyone look slightly green. Life-changing conversations that made none of that matter.

Life can feel like a roadside diner long past its prime. The health certificate is yellowed and forgotten, the booths are patched with duct tape, and the jukebox only works if you smack it just right. Everything looks worn down, barely holding together. Yet even there, in places that seem overlooked and broken, God still shows up.

Our group: Me. Mike, former Army Ranger with a Purple Heart and PTSD that made him jump whenever someone dropped a fork. Tony, recovering alcoholic who'd been sober seven years but still introduced himself as an alcoholic because "forgetting what you are is the first step to becoming it again." Eduardo, construction foreman whose wife left him after their daughter died of leukemia. And Tom, the giant former NFL prospect I mentioned earlier.

We called ourselves the Thursday Morning Failures Club. Not officially. That's just what Mike wrote on his coffee cup one morning, and it stuck.

One morning, after six months of showing up but never really sharing, I finally told them about the Caribbean. The accident. The guilt that felt like a physical weight on my chest. The way I couldn't drive at dusk without my hands shaking. You know what happened? Three other guys had similar stories:

Mike had killed someone in Iraq, friendly fire incident that was nobody's fault but haunted him every day. Tony had caused a drunk driving accident twenty years earlier that killed a mother of three. Eduardo's construction site accident had claimed a worker's life due to a decision he'd made about safety equipment.

Mike was the first to speak after I shared. "Rockwell," he always used last names, military habit, "you know what the difference is between us and everybody else?" He pointed around the diner at the normal people eating normal breakfasts. "We know what it costs. Every breath we take was paid for by someone else's last one. That knowledge either destroys you or transforms you. No middle ground."

We weren't alone. We were a brotherhood of men carrying invisible corpses, and somehow, sharing the weight made it bearable.

"Carry each other's burdens, and in this way you will fulfill the law of Christ" (Galatians 6:2, NIV). The early church didn't have programs, buildings, or worship bands. They had each other. We've complicated something that was meant to be simple: showing up for each other.

Step 5: Pursue Purpose in Pain

This is where it gets interesting. Not comfortable. Not easy. Interesting.

March 2015. Hong Kong. My friend Natalya had been bugging me for weeks to meet this girl from her church. I was 43, twice divorced, carrying enough baggage to fill a cargo plane. But I went to a church gathering to make Natalya stop asking.

The gathering was in someone's apartment in Wan Chai. Thirty-second floor, view of the harbor that would cost you seven figures in Manhattan. Belonged to some Russian oligarch's kid who'd found Jesus and was trying to spend daddy's money on something meaningful.

I wore my best shirt, the one clean enough to pass at first glance. But I still felt out of place, like I'd wandered in from the wrong side of town. Everyone else looked like they'd been handpicked for Beautiful Christians Monthly.

I finally met her. Stefaniya wasn't like anyone else I'd ever known. Within two weeks, I was spilling everything. We were in a cramped ramen shop in Causeway Bay, the kind where you buy your ticket from a vending machine and sit shoulder-to-shoulder with strangers. I sat there crying into my bowl, telling a woman I barely knew my darkest moments, and she just listened. No fixing. No clichés. Just the grace of someone willing to hold my pain.

She said, "So God's not finished with you yet."

That floored me. Not "You're broken." Not "You need therapy" (though I did). Not "I can fix you." Just acknowledgment that I was still under construction, that the story wasn't over, that God was still writing.

"And we know that in all things God works for the good of those who love him" (Romans 8:28, NIV). I used to hate that verse. How is killing someone "good"? How are failed marriages "good"? How is depression that makes you want to stop existing "good"?

But maybe, just maybe, it's not saying the things themselves are good. Maybe it's saying that God can work through anything—even our worst moments—to create something meaningful. Not meaningful enough to justify the pain, but meaningful enough to redeem it.

The Hidden Cost of Unprocessed Pain

Here's something I wish someone had told me in that Caribbean police station: every day you don't deal with your pain costs you weeks, months, maybe years down the road. It's like compound interest, but in reverse. The longer you let it sit, the more expensive it becomes.

I did the math once. Sitting in an airport lounge in Dubai, flight delayed, nothing to do but think. Twenty years of running from pain. Of pretending busyness was healing. Of mistaking motion for progress.

It looked something like this:

- Therapy avoided: $200 a week × 52 weeks × 20 years = $208,000

- Alcohol to numb: $50 a week × 52 weeks × 20 years = $52,000

- Failed relationships: Two divorces at roughly $30,000 each = $60,000

- Miles flown running from stillness: 2.7 million miles × $0.40 a mile = $1,080,000

- Actual therapy when I finally broke: $300 a week × 2 years = $31,200

Total cost of avoiding $208,000 worth of healing: $1,431,200.

Turns out the pain wasn't the expensive part. The running was.

That's not counting the intangibles. The relationships that died from neglect. The opportunities missed while I was busy running. The decades of sleep lost to 3 AM guilt sessions.

I used to think God was waiting for me at the finish line—arms crossed, checking the clock, disappointed I took the long way. I was wrong. He was in every detour, every night I tried to drink myself quiet, every mile I flew trying not to feel.

Grace doesn't charge by the hour. It waits.

And when I finally stopped running, I realized what I'd been avoiding all along wasn't punishment. It was restoration. God wasn't asking me to pay for what I'd done; He was inviting me to stop paying for what I refused to surrender.

Some debts you settle by finally letting go.

I spent approximately 15,000 hours, that's nearly two full years of wake time, running from pain I could have faced in a month. Flying between continents, building businesses as distractions, creating elaborate life structures to avoid one simple truth: I needed to grieve. I needed to mourn not just the man who died, but the version of myself that died that night, too, the innocent one who'd never been responsible for ending a life.

Every hour you invest in processing pain today saves you days of dysfunction tomorrow. That's kingdom economics right there.

Living It Out: The Daily Grind of Faith Through Pain

Tuesday morning, 6:47 AM. Alex is having a meltdown because his brother Evan looked at his waffle wrong. My two-year-old Olivia is painting the wall with yogurt, organic, of course, because even our messes are high-quality. Stefaniya's trying to get everyone ready for school while maintaining the patience of a saint. And I'm standing there, coffee in hand, thinking about that family in the Caribbean.

The waffle in question had syrup in every single square. Alex's particular about syrup distribution. Takes him ten minutes to fill each square precisely. Evan looked at it and said, "That's weird."

Nuclear meltdown. DEFCON 1. The neighbors probably think we're torturing someone.

I couldn't stop thinking about who that man might have left behind. Maybe a wife, maybe a child, or maybe no one at all. Somewhere, a kitchen light could still be burning, dinner sitting cold on the table, waiting for a man who never walked through the door. The night around me was heavy and still, broken only by the hum of insects, and none of it offered an answer.

Did they have mornings like this? Chaos and waffles and life happening all at once? Did that man have children who argued over breakfast? A wife who juggled too many things? A normal Tuesday that he assumed would be followed by a normal Wednesday.

The guilt doesn't vanish because you find faith. Let me be crystal clear about that. It transforms, but it doesn't disappear. It becomes a reminder of grace. Of the weight of our choices. Of our desperate need for something bigger than ourselves. Of the fact that life is fragile and precious and can end in an instant.

And somehow, in ways I'll never fully understand, God still uses even our worst moments. Not causes them. Not celebrates them. But uses them. Redeems them. Transforms them from pure pain into purposeful pain.

Last week, a guy at church asked me to talk to his son. Kid's nineteen, just caused a car accident that paralyzed someone. Can't stop replaying it. Can't sleep. Can't eat. Can't understand how God could let it happen.

We met in a noisy café, the hiss of steam and clatter of cups filling the air. He asked only for water. And sitting there, I remembered how often God uses the simplest things to quench what we really thirst for. I recognized the look, that thousand-yard stare of someone whose life has been bifurcated into before and after.

"Does it get better?" he asked.

"No," I said. "It gets different. The weight doesn't go away, but you get stronger. And eventually, God shows you how to use that strength to help others carry their weight."

He started crying. Right there in the café, with hipsters typing novels and moms discussing school drama. And I let him. Because sometimes the most spiritual thing you can do is cry in a café.

YOUR NEXT STEP

Set aside one hour this week, just one, to honestly face something you've been avoiding. Write it out in detail. Not the version you've been telling people. The real version. The ugly version. The version that makes you question God's goodness.

Then find one person—a counselor, a pastor, a trusted friend—and share the real version with them. Watch what happens when you stop carrying alone what was never meant to be carried alone.

Here's what will actually happen: you'll schedule the hour, then find seventeen things that suddenly need doing. The garage needs organizing. The car needs washing. Your sock drawer requires immediate attention.

Do it anyway. Set a timer. Sixty minutes. Write until the timer goes off or until you run out of tears, whichever comes first.

Then make the call. Send the text. Schedule the appointment. The anticipation will be worse than the actual sharing. It always is.

Remember: your pain isn't punishment. Your suffering isn't meaningless. Your worst moment might become the foundation for your greatest ministry. But first, you have to stop running and start processing.

One hour today saves countless hours tomorrow. Your pain, processed and surrendered, becomes someone else's hope. That's the economy of the Kingdom. That's how God writes redemption stories. Even yours. Especially yours.

CHAPTER FOUR

Sacred Reflection

Practical Tools for Hearing God in Hard Times

Three AM. That's when God and I have our best conversations. Not because I'm super religious, but because that's when my four-year-old, Evan, decides nightmares are real and only Daddy can fix them. Last Tuesday, holding him while he shook and sobbed about monsters that seemed absolutely real to his young mind, I whispered the prayer my aunt taught me in her kitchen back in Stephenville when I was about his age: *'Jesus, be near.'*

That night, Evan dreamed of wolves. Not cartoon ones. Real ones, with yellow eyes and dripping teeth. He was wearing his Paw Patrol pajamas, Marshall the fire dog grinning on the shirt. The irony wasn't lost on me: a boy, terrified, while wearing clothes meant to remind him of courage. His little body burned against mine, furnace-hot the way only a crying four-year-old can be, and I wondered if it was a fever or just the sheer intensity of being that young.

"They were in our backyard, Daddy. Looking in the window."

"But we don't have wolves in Texas, buddy. Just coyotes, and they're scared of people."

"These wolves weren't scared."

At 3 AM, logic doesn't work on four-year-olds. Or on fifty-three-year-olds wrestling with God, for that matter.

75

Simple words. Three syllables. But isn't that what we all need when life gets heavy? Not theological explanations. Not five-point sermons. Just the presence of someone who loves us in the darkness.

My aunt—she was more like a grandmother to me—had this way of praying that made God feel like He was sitting at the kitchen table with us. She'd be making biscuits from scratch, flour dusting everything, including her glasses, and she'd talk to God like He was helping her measure ingredients. "Lord, Simon's having a hard time at school. You know those boys are picking on him. Give him the strength to face tomorrow. And maybe make those boys' consciences work overtime tonight."

Aunt Gee's kitchen in Stephenville, Texas, was about the size of a walk-in closet. Harvest gold appliances from 1973. Linoleum floor that peeled at the corners. But that kitchen produced more prayers and biscuits than any cathedral I've been in since. She had this wooden spoon, handle worn smooth from fifty years of stirring, that she'd wave around while praying like she was conducting God's orchestra.

"Lord, you know the Hendricks boy is back on the drugs. His mama's heart is breaking. Send someone to knock sense into that child. And if nobody's available, I'll do it myself with this here spoon."

She died when I was thirty-two, a stroke while making Sunday dinner. My uncle found her on the kitchen floor, roast still in the oven, timer going off. At her funeral, seventeen people told stories about her praying for them in that same kitchen. The pastor said she had a direct line to God. I think she just knew His address was wherever people were hurting.

After she was gone, I kept wondering what she'd found in those prayers, how someone could touch heaven in an ordinary kitchen.

Three years later, still chasing that kind of faith, I found myself in Jerusalem during Easter. I keep a photo on my desk from that trip: my hand pressed against the Western Wall; prayer notes wedged into every crack around me like desperate messages in bottles tossed into a stone sea. That trip changed everything. Standing where Jesus walked, touching stones that had witnessed miracles, I felt both incredibly small and inexplicably loved.

The tour guide kept rushing us, "Fifteen more minutes, then we move to the next site!" but I couldn't move. Something in those ancient stones whispered, Stay.

The tour was "Walking Where Jesus Walked," $3,200 for ten days, including airfare from Houston. Highway robbery, but I needed to go. Needed to see if standing on holy ground would make me feel less like damaged goods. The group was mostly retired Baptists from Alabama who kept trying to save my soul, not knowing it was already saved, just severely dented.

The Western Wall is smaller than you expect. All those photos make it look massive. In person, it's human-scaled. Touchable. The stones are worn smooth from millions of hands over centuries, polished by the oil of desperate palms pressing prayers into rock.

My prayer, written on International Convention Center stationery (I'd been there for InnoTech 2005): "God, I killed someone. Can You still use me?" Folded seven times until it was small enough to wedge between stones that had been there since before Christ.

The businessman next to me, Swiss watch, Italian suit, was sobbing so hard his shoulders shook. His prayer fell out when he pulled back from the wall. Three words: "Please let her live." All the money in the world, and he was just another broken person begging God for a miracle.

Twenty minutes of tourists flowing around me like water around a rock while I stood there, a grown man crying at a wall, finally understanding what it means to bring your broken pieces to God. Not your Sunday best. Not your cleaned-up testimony. Your actual broken pieces, sharp edges, and all.

The Hidden Power of Introspection in Strengthening Your Faith

My second marriage ended on Thursday. I remember because Thursdays were taco night, and I was standing in a Kowloon grocery store, holding a packet of Old El Paso seasoning that I'd paid too much for at the import shop, when I realized I'd never make tacos in that apartment again. My wife, who is now my ex-wife, had already moved back to the States. The apartment felt like a museum of a life that no longer existed. Her coffee mug still by the sink. Her pillow still indented on her side of the bed. But her presence was gone, like she'd been erased from space but left her shadow.

ParknShop in Tsim Sha Tsui. The Old El Paso kit was 62 Hong Kong dollars, about $8 US dollars, for taco shells that were probably manufactured during the Clinton administration. But Thursday was taco night. Had been for three years. Even when Josephine and I were barely speaking, we'd sit at our tiny IKEA table and crunch through silence.

Josephine, I can say her name now without my chest tightening, had left a Post-it on the fridge: "Water the plant." That was it. Three years of marriage reduced to care instructions for a spider plant that was already half-dead from neglect. The plant survived longer than the marriage, which feels like a metaphor for something, though I'm not sure what.

The apartment was 650 square feet, which is spacious by Hong Kong standards. Cost me 18,000 HKD a month, about $2,300 US. Most expensive storage unit for emotional baggage ever rented.

Weird what sticks with you in moments of ending. Not the big things, the lawyers, the papers, the division of assets. But the small stuff. Taco seasoning. The absence of her laugh. The way the apartment echoed now when I walked.

That night, I did something I hadn't done in years. Really prayed. Not the "bless this food" kind that had become rote. Not the emergency "help me God" prayers I'd perfected during turbulence or tough business negotiations. I mean the messy, angry, confused kind where you're not even sure God wants to hear what you have to say.

I sat on the floor of that empty apartment. I had furniture, but somehow the floor felt more appropriate for the kind of conversation I needed to have. The hardwood was cold against my palms as I pressed them down, trying to ground myself in something solid while everything else felt like it was floating away.

The floor was that fake wood laminate that looks good in photos but feels like plastic under your hands. I could hear my upstairs neighbor practicing violin badly. Sounded like someone torturing a cat in B-flat. The couple next door was arguing in Cantonese. The only word I understood was the English profanity they kept dropping in for emphasis.

"Are You there?" I said out loud to the empty room. "Because I can't tell anymore. I've done everything I thought You wanted. Got baptized—twice, actually. Served in church leadership. Gave even when money was tight. Not because I believed You still required a tenth, since Christ fulfilled the old law (Romans 10:4), but because generosity is how grace breathes. The New Testament doesn't set a percentage; it sets a posture. 'Each of you should give what you have decided in your heart to give, not reluctantly or under compulsion, for God loves a cheerful giver' (2 Corinthians 9:7).

"I tried to live that way—to give freely, love deeply, and serve humbly. Tried to be a good husband, too. Failed twice at that, apparently. So, either You're not there, or You're not who I thought You were, or I'm so broken that even You can't fix me."

The silence that answered felt different than before. Not empty silence. Waiting silence. Like when a counselor lets you sit with what you just said until you hear it yourself.

Then my phone buzzed. Text from my mother back in Texas: "Praying for you tonight. Don't know why, but you're on my heart."

2:47 AM Hong Kong time. 12:47 PM Texas time. Mom was probably at Luby's having her Thursday cafeteria lunch, always the fish, always the green beans, always the chess pie, when God apparently interrupted her routine to mention her mess of a son 8,346 miles away.

I grabbed a notebook from the 7-Eleven down the street. Nothing fancy. Blue cover, cheap paper that bled through if you pressed too hard with a pen. My first entry? Three words that felt like they weighed a thousand pounds:

"Still here, God."

Was it a statement? A question? A challenge? Honestly, all three. After twenty years of running from the accident, two failed marriages, and more mistakes than I could count on both hands, somehow, I was

80

still breathing. Still inexplicably held by grace I couldn't earn or explain.

The Art of Prayer Journaling in a Digital Age

That notebook from 7-Eleven cost 12 Hong Kong dollars. Still have it. Water damage from when I spilled San Miguel on it. Coffee rings on most pages like passport stamps from my daily ritual of caffeine and crisis. Tear stains that made the ink run, turning some prayers into abstract art. Page 73 has dried ramen noodles stuck to it from when I tried to journal while eating. Multi-tasking my misery.

What surprised me most about keeping a prayer journal was this: the first fifty pages will probably make you cringe when you read them later. Mine did. Reading back through those early entries from Kowloon feels like listening to voicemails from a different person, angry, entitled, asking God why He let me mess up instead of asking why I kept choosing the mess.

Page 1: "God, where are You?" Page 7: "I can't do this anymore." Page 15: "Why did You let me marry her if You knew it would end?" Page 23: "I hate who I've become." Page 31: "Maybe You're not real." Page 38: "If You're real, I need a sign. Anything." Page 44: "The ramen shop owner smiled at me today. Was that You?"

But somewhere around page 51, something shifted. I stopped performing for God and started talking to Him. No more King James' language that I thought made prayers holier. No more trying to sound spiritual. Just raw honesty:

Page 51, March 14, 2013, 11:47 PM: "God, I'm drunk again. Not fall-down drunk. Functional drunk. The kind where I can still type emails and appear normal on video calls, but I'm numb enough not to feel the weight. I know this isn't the answer. But I don't know what is.

Help me want to stop.

P.S. The 7-Eleven clerk, Amy (not her real name, guaranteed), gave me a look tonight. Not judgment. Pity. Which is worse."

Page 52, March 22, 2013, 6:23 AM: "Hungover. Again. Can see Lion Rock through my window for the first time in weeks. Clear day. It looks like You, solid, unmovable, there even when clouds hide it. Am I the clouds? Probably."

Page 67, April 2, 2013, 3:15 PM: "That girl at the convenience store smiled at me today when I couldn't figure out the right change. Different girl. Not Amy. This one actually seemed happy. First genuine human kindness I've felt in weeks. Was that You? Using a 7-Eleven clerk to remind me I'm still human?"

I started noticing things. Small things. The elderly man at the wet market who saw my Cantonese falter, and with quiet patience, picked the right coins from my palm while the line behind us grew restless. On clear mornings, Lion Rock emerged through the haze beyond my office window, like God pulling back a curtain to remind me that beauty still existed. Later, as I walked through Kowloon, bougainvillea petals scattered across the pavement, bright pink against gray concrete. They never stayed long, carried off by wind or crushed underfoot, each one a quiet reminder that beautiful things don't last forever. And maybe that's what makes them beautiful.

Page 89, May 1, 2013, 2:00 AM: "Can't sleep. Watching the city from my window. Hong Kong never stops. Like anxiety. Like guilt. Like Your grace, apparently, since I'm still here despite everything. The neon signs across the harbor are reflecting on the water, broken light dancing on black waves. Broken but still beautiful. Is that Your point?"

Now? I use both analog and digital. My leather journal, an

anniversary gift from Stefaniya, who knows me better than I deserve, lives on my nightstand for those 3 AM moments when my son's nightmares become doorways to deeper conversations with God. My phone app catches prayers in traffic, usually voice memos that start with "Okay God, here's what's on my mind..." while I'm stuck on the highway watching brake lights stretch to the horizon.

Not pretty. Not poetic. Just real.

When You Can't Find Words (Borrowed Prayers for Broken People)

Sometimes we need training wheels. Sometimes the pain is so acute or the numbness so complete that we can't form our own words. That's okay. That's why God gave us the Psalms, the Lord's Prayer, and each other. Here are actual prayers from my journal, offered like tools in a toolbox for when you can't build your own:

I started collecting these like some people collect baseball cards. Other people's prayers that worked when mine wouldn't. Written on index cards, napkins, receipts, whatever was handy when I heard something that made my soul say "yes, that."

The 3 AM Panic Prayer (Used this 47 times according to my journal): "God, I can't breathe. The weight is too heavy. I don't need answers right now. I don't need to understand Your plan. I just need You to sit with me in this. Like You sat with Mary and Martha when Lazarus died. Like You wept even though You knew You were about to raise him. Sit with me in this pain before You do anything with it."

First used: March 27, 2013, Hong Kong apartment, after a nightmare about the accident. Last used: Last Thursday, in my garage, after Alex asked why people die.

The Parenting Failure Prayer (This one's getting worn out): "Lord, I raised my voice again. Not in anger, exactly, just frustration that got too loud. I never heard my dad yell at me, but I remember the sound of him and Mom arguing, voices sharp enough to fill the house. I remember his belt, too, how I'd start crying before it ever landed. The waiting was worse than the sting. I swore I'd never pass that fear on to my kids. Yet tonight, when I shouted, I saw the same flinch I used to feel.

Show them Your love through my flaws. Teach me to speak with patience instead of power. Help me to discipline with understanding, not fear. And when I fail again, and I will, help me to apologize faster and love louder."

I used to think discipline meant control. Now I know it's about guidance and grace. My father did what he knew, and I've come to believe he loved me the best way he could. But God parents differently. He doesn't reach for the belt or raise His voice. He corrects with truth, but He does it through love. Scripture says, *"The Lord is compassionate and gracious, slow to anger, abounding in love"* (Psalm 103:8).

That's the kind of parent I want to be, slow to anger, quick to listen, steady enough that my kids never have to wonder whether love is still in the room after a hard moment.

One night, I used the "Parenting Failure Prayer" after I lost it on Alex for spilling grape juice on my laptop. Not just any laptop, the one with the quarterly report I hadn't backed up. He was trying to bring me juice because I looked tired. Kid tries to love me, and I roar at him like he committed a felony. Spent an hour holding him while he cried, then another hour after he fell asleep, feeling guilty.

The Work Stress Prayer (Written on a Singapore Airlines napkin):

"Jesus, this deal is falling apart. Three months of negotiation, about to collapse. I've done everything I know to do. If this is You closing a door, help me trust. If it's You testing faith, help me stand. If it's just life in a broken world, help me navigate. And help me remember that my worth isn't tied to this outcome."

Used when the Malaysian petroleum contract fell through. Three million dollars, gone because someone's nephew needed a job. Also used when the Hong Kong merger collapsed. And when that client in Dallas decided to go with my competitor who promised impossible things.

The Gratitude Struggle Prayer (Written during the worst of the depression): "God, I'm supposed to be grateful, but I'm just angry. Thank you for not requiring perfect prayers. Thank you for including angry Psalms in Your Word. Thank you for not smiting me when I doubt You. Help me find one small thing today. Just one. Start there."

This one came from my therapist, Dr. Evelyn Hart, who charged $200 an hour to tell me things I already knew but needed to hear from someone with credentials. Her private practice sat in a quiet suite on Westheimer, tucked between high-end boutiques and a café that always smelled like croissants and money. It wasn't the kind of place you'd expect transformation to happen. Everything was polished, soft lighting, white orchids, and leather chairs that looked like they'd never seen a bad day.

"Gratitude isn't feeling grateful," she said during session number twelve. "It's choosing to look for something worth acknowledging even when everything feels worthless."

"That's the dumbest thing I've ever heard," I told her.

"That's why you need to try it," she said.

85

She was right. I hate when therapists are right.

The Marriage Prayer (Stefaniya made me write this on an index card): "Lord, help me love Stefaniya like You love the church. When I want to be right, help me choose to be kind instead. When I want to withdraw, help me lean in. When I want to keep score, help me throw away the scorecard. She deserves better than what I am, but help me become what she deserves."

I keep this card in my wallet, behind my driver's license. It's worn soft now, ink faded, corner torn from the time I pulled it out too fast during an argument and used it like a white flag. Stefaniya laughed, the first time I'd heard her laugh during a fight. "You're literally pulling out a prayer card in the middle of our argument?" she asked. "Yes," I said. "I'm out of other options." We ended up praying together instead of fighting. Still had to discuss the budget, but at least we did it without drawing blood.

Self-Assessment as a Spiritual Mirror

King David had it right: "Search me, God, and know my heart; test me and know my anxious thoughts" (Psalm 139:23, NIV). Though I bet David didn't have to do his soul-searching while assembling IKEA furniture at midnight because the baby's crib arrived in 47 pieces with instructions that looked like hieroglyphics.

The SUNDVIK crib. "Easy assembly in 30 minutes!" the website promised. Three hours later, at 1 AM, eight months pregnant, Stefaniya was watching from the doorway while I tried not to curse in front of the baby she was carrying. I had the frame upside down for the first hour. The Allen wrench, that cursed piece of Swedish engineering, stripped two screws before I figured out I was turning it the wrong way.

"Maybe we should pray about it," Stefaniya suggested when she found me sitting on the floor, surrounded by wooden pieces like I was building a Viking funeral pyre.

"God doesn't care about IKEA furniture," I said.

"God cares about everything that makes you this angry," she replied.

We prayed. The crib still took another hour, but I stopped wanting to burn it.

Every quarter, I do what I call a spiritual audit. Yeah, it sounds corporate because old consulting habits die hard. But King David did it, read the Psalms. Paul did it, read 2 Corinthians. Even Jesus did it in the garden of Gethsemane. Sometimes you need to take inventory of your soul.

Here's what it really looks like: Black coffee, always too strong because I use twice the recommended grounds. My garage corner before the house wakes up, usually 5 AM, sometimes earlier if anxiety is my alarm clock. And I ask myself the questions I usually avoid:

Last quarter's audit, September 2023. Written on the back of Alex's school lunch menu because I forgot my journal:

Where did fear win this week?

• Tuesday: Stayed silent when I felt the Spirit nudging me to speak hope into someone's bad day. I told myself it wasn't the right time.

• Wednesday: Opened my Bible, read three verses, then scrolled my phone for twenty minutes. Said I was "unwinding."

• Friday: Told my wife I was fine when I wasn't. Fear of being seen still wears the mask of strength.

- Sunday: Sat through worship, thinking about bills instead of grace.

- When did I choose comfort over obedience?

- Slept through the men's prayer breakfast, third week in a row. Told myself God and I could talk later.

- Spent two hours scrolling my phone instead of reading Scripture. Called it "staying informed."

- Let Netflix play the next episode instead of having the complicated conversation with Stefaniya about our weekly budget. Funny how silence feels easier than honesty when money is involved.

What prayers am I still too scared to pray? The big one: "God, use my story, all of it, even the parts I wish had never happened, for Your glory." Because what if He actually does? What if He asks me to speak openly about the worst night of my life? What if the purpose of pain isn't to bury it, but to let it become light for someone else's darkness?

There are moments I still replay in my head, faces I'll never forget, questions I'll never be able to answer. Sometimes, late at night, I wonder what redemption looks like when you can't undo the damage. I've written a hundred letters in my mind, not to send, but to understand.

How did I love poorly? And more importantly, who did I fail to love at all?

- My neighbor Jim, who keeps asking me to help fix his fence. It would take two hours. I've been "too busy" for the past 6 months.

- The homeless vet at the I-10 underpass. I see him every morning. I've given him money exactly once.

- Stefaniya was telling me about her day, and I nodded in all the right places while thinking about tomorrow's to-do list. Love isn't just presence; it's attention. Missed that one.

Where do I need to actually repent? Not just feel bad. Not just promise to "do better." But actually, turn around and walk in the other direction. The drinking that's creeping back. The anger that's becoming my default. The pride that whispers I've earned God's favor through suffering.

Last quarter's audit revealed something painful: I'd been so focused on not failing at marriage number three that I'd forgotten actually to be present in it. I was performing the role of "good husband" rather than being one. Stefaniya didn't need a perfect husband. She needed the imperfect one who was actually there, not constantly looking over his shoulder at past failures or ahead to potential problems.

Documenting Divine Fingerprints

A little over a year ago, Stefaniya was bleeding. Twenty weeks pregnant with our third child, and the ultrasound tech's face told us everything before she said a word. That particular expression medical professionals get when they're trying to figure out how to deliver devastating news. I've seen it before, in the Caribbean, in divorce lawyers' offices, in oncology wards.

HCA Houston Healthcare, Room 214, in February 2024, 12:47 AM. I know the exact time because I was staring at the clock, thinking how normal it looked while our world was potentially ending. The ultrasound tech was young, maybe twenty-five, with a butterfly tattoo on her wrist that she kept trying to hide under her scrubs.

"I need to get the doctor," she said. Those six words that every pregnant woman fears.

The gel on Stefaniya's belly was already starting to dry, pulling at her skin. She was gripping my hand so hard I lost feeling in my fingers. I didn't care. I would have let her break every bone if it would have helped.

I gripped Stefaniya's hand hard enough to hurt, trying to channel strength I didn't have while internally screaming at God: "Not again. After everything, not this. Haven't we paid enough? Haven't we suffered enough? What more do You want from us?"

The tech left to get the doctor. Those minutes stretched like hours. Stefaniya was praying in Ukrainian, tears running down her face onto that crinkly paper they put on examination tables. I was bargaining with God in my head, offering anything, my business, my health, my life, in exchange for that heartbeat.

Dr. Martinez came in twelve minutes later. I know because I counted every second. She didn't say anything at first, just moved the ultrasound wand with the kind of precision that comes from twenty years of looking for problems. The screen was turned toward her, away from us. Stefaniya had stopped praying and was breathing—shallow, scared breaths, as if she were afraid deep breathing might disturb whatever was happening inside her.

Then the doctor adjusted the screen, moved the wand slightly, and changed the angle. A flutter. Tiny, persistent, impossible to miss.

A heartbeat.

"There," she said, pointing to the screen. "The baby moved into a difficult position, but there's the heartbeat. Strong. Steady. Everything looks fine."

142 beats per minute. I made her count it twice. Then asked the tech to count it. Then counted it myself on the screen. 142 beautiful beats per minute. Our daughter, Olivia, being dramatic before she was even born.

I have that ultrasound image saved on my phone. Not in some folder, but as my lock screen for six months. Some people think that's morbid, keeping a picture from the worst day that became the best day. But when Samuel set up that stone and called it Ebenezer, "Thus far the Lord has helped us" (1 Samuel 7:12, NIV), he was doing the same thing. Creating a monument to remember.

My Ebenezer stones aren't very Instagram-worthy:

• A business card from the attorney who handled my first divorce (reminds me that grace is bigger than failure)

• The receipt from the Hong Kong restaurant where I first saw Stefaniya laugh, really laugh, the kind where she snorted and then covered her mouth, embarrassed (HK$347.50 for ramen and possibility)

• A photo of the Western Wall with my prayer still wedged between the stones

• My kids' hospital bracelets (all three, including the scary one from when Alex had seizures at six months)

• A coffee-stained napkin from that Denny's where Dolores told me about survivor's guilt being love with nowhere to go

Also: a rock from the Caribbean. Yeah, I went back. 2018. I arranged a business trip to pass through that island. I stood at the spot where it happened. It's been developed now, a shopping center where the empty road used to be—progress covering history. But I found a rock from the old shoulder of the road, a smooth black volcanic stone about the size of a quarter. I keep it in my desk drawer. Sometimes I hold it when I pray, remembering that God was there too that night—having the one who fell, even as I was left standing.

I used to think that rock was a reminder of guilt. Now I see it differently. It's a reminder that grace reaches even the places we wish we could forget. That God's mercy doesn't stay at the altar; it walks the old roads with us.

These aren't lucky charms or superstitious totems. They're reminders that God shows up. Especially when we think He won't. Particularly in places we'd never expect. Through people we'd never choose. In ways we'd never imagine.

Creating Sacred Space in a Busy World

After Hong Kong, when we moved back to Texas, we bought a house with a garage, which I immediately claimed. Stefaniya calls it my "man cave," but really, it's my prayer closet. One corner has a beat-up chair from Goodwill that's held together with duct tape and hope. A wobbly table I built myself that keeps my coffee mug perfectly, because I built it specifically for that purpose. And a cross my mother gave me before she passed, simple wood, nothing ornate, but it was on her bedside table for forty years.

The chair cost $15 at the Goodwill on Interstate 45. Green pleather that's cracked like a road map of Texas. The left armrest is completely bare, foam exposed, from where I rest my arm during long prayer sessions. The table is made from a door I found on bulk trash day and four legs from different furniture pieces. It lists to the right, so I shimmed it with a folded bulletin from church, the one where they announced we were doing a series on suffering. Seemed appropriate.

Nothing Pinterest-worthy. Everything sacred.

Jesus said, "When you pray, go into your room, close the door and pray to your Father, who is unseen" (Matthew 6:6, NIV). He wasn't giving decorating tips. He was talking about intentionality. About creating space where you can be honest with God without performing for anyone.

But here's the thing, sacred space isn't always a place. Sometimes it's a time. Sometimes it's a practice. Sometimes it's just the decision to turn off the radio during your commute and talk to God instead.

My sacred spaces include:

The garage prayer corner: Best for ugly crying and wrestling matches with God. The concrete floor has absorbed more tears than I can count. The walls have heard confessions I've never voiced to another human. This is where I go when I need to yell at God, and He's gracious enough to let me.

The temperature in there reaches 104°F in August. I sweat out prayers like a sauna for the soul. In February, it's 38°F and I can see my breath, prayers visible like incense. The extremes feel appropriate for extreme conversations with the Almighty.

My truck: More honest conversations with God happen in my 2018 Silverado than anywhere else. Something about driving, eyes on the road, hands on the wheel, frees my mouth to say things I couldn't say looking at a cross. Plus, nobody can hear you scream on I-35.

The back porch at sunrise: Before the neighbors start their leaf blowers, before the kids wake up, before the day's demands start their assault. Just me, coffee, and God watching the world wake up. This is where gratitude feels most natural.

Walking the neighborhood while the kids bike: Multitasking at its spiritual finest. "God, help me be patient," as Alex crashes his bike for the third time. "God, give me wisdom," as Evan asks why some people don't have homes. "God, help me be present" as I resist checking my phone.

Last week, during our walk, Alex asked, "Dad, does God ever get tired of listening to us?"

"No, buddy. Never."

"Even when we ask for the same thing over and over?"

"Especially then."

"Good. Because I'm going to keep asking for a dog."

The space matters less than the showing up. God met Moses in a bush. Elijah in a cave. Jonah in a fish. Paul in a prison. He can meet you in a minivan during soccer practice or a bathroom stall during your lunch break.

When Reflection Meets Real Life

Last month, our middle child had a night terror. If you've never experienced one, imagine your child trapped in a nightmare they can't wake up from. Screaming, thrashing, completely unreachable. Their eyes are open, but they're not seeing you. They're seeing whatever horror their mind has conjured, and you can't pull them out of it.

Evan, our four-year-old. 2:17 AM. His scream could peel paint. He was fighting invisible enemies, throwing punches at the air, crying about "the bad birds" that were trying to take him. His pajamas were soaked with sweat. His little face contorted in terror, and I couldn't fix itStefaniya tried singing. I tried holding him. Alex came in crying because the screaming scared him. Olivia slept through it because that baby could sleep through Armageddon.

As I held Evan, his little body rigid with fear, his screams primal and desperate, I found myself praying the Jesus Prayer: "Lord Jesus Christ, Son of God, have mercy on me, a sinner." Over and over, like a heartbeat, like a lifeline, like a parent rocking a child. The ancient rhythm of it, repeated by millions of believers over centuries, connected me to something bigger than my inadequacy as a father.

"Lord Jesus Christ" (acknowledging who He is), "Son of God" (acknowledging His divinity), "Have mercy on me" (acknowledging my need), "A sinner" (acknowledging my reality).

Twenty-three minutes. That's how long the night terror lasted. I know because I watched the clock the entire time, praying that prayer probably a hundred times. When Evan finally collapsed into normal sleep, his body going limp like someone had cut his strings, I kept praying it. For him. For me. For every parent who's ever held a terrified child and felt utterly powerless.

That's when it clicked. This is the real work of faith. Not the Instagram-worthy quiet time with fair-trade coffee and a leather journal. Not the highlighted Bible with color-coded tabs. But meeting God in the mess. In the hospital rooms where prayers feel pointless. In the divorce papers that mock your promises. In the custody battles that break your heart. In the 3 AM terror when all you have is an ancient prayer and a love bigger than fear.

Building Resilience Through Reflection

You want to know the truth about resilience? It's not built on victories. It's built in the moments after defeat when you choose to stand up again. It's built in the reflection that happens between the falling and the rising.

My 2015 journal, right before meeting Stefaniya, is painful to read. Pages of bargaining with God: "If You just give me one more chance at love..." "If You help me find the right woman..." "If You fix this loneliness..." As if God was a cosmic vending machine and I just needed the right combination of coins.

February 14, 2015. Valentine's Day. Alone in Hong Kong. Wrote this gem: "God, I'll go to church every Sunday. I'll tithe 15%. I'll stop drinking. I'll read through the Bible in a year. Just send me someone who can love me despite what I've done."

Like God needed my resume of religious activities. Like He was up there with a checklist: "Well, Simon's offering 15% now instead of 10%. Better send him a wife."

But looking back now, I can see Him working in the waiting. Every wrong turn in Hong Kong led me closer to that Slavic church where Natalya would introduce me to my wife. Every failed relationship taught me what real love wasn't, preparing me to recognize what it was. Every night of loneliness carved out space for the companionship that was coming.

Resilience isn't about being strong enough to never fall. It's about developing the muscle memory of getting back up. It's about learning to see God's hand in the aftermath, even when you couldn't see it in the impact.

There's a note in my journal from March 1, 2015, two weeks before I met Stefaniya: "God feels silent. But maybe silence isn't absence. Maybe He's just waiting for me to stop talking long enough to listen."

Turns out, He was.

YOUR NEXT STEP

Tomorrow morning, before checking your phone, before the day's demands start shouting, write three things. Anything. Could be gratitude: "Coffee exists." Could be complaint: "Still angry about yesterday." Could be a question: "Where are you in this mess?"

In reality, this is what will occur: Your alarm will go off. You'll reach for your phone. Stop. Put it down. Grab whatever's nearby: a napkin, a receipt, or your kid's construction paper. Write three things. They don't have to be profound. They don't have to be spiritual. They just have to be honest.

My three things this morning:

1. Scared about the biopsy results

2. Alex hugged me for no reason yesterday

3. Where are You in my fear?

That's it. Thirty seconds. But it's thirty seconds of choosing to turn toward God instead of toward the noise.

Just start the conversation. God's waiting to meet you in the rough, where the real you lives, not in the sanitized clean room. He can handle your doubts, your anger, your questions. He's big enough for all of it.

And keep writing, every day. Watch what happens when you create space for honest conversation with the Creator of the universe. You might be surprised to find He's been trying to talk to you all along.

Final thought: I still wake up at 3 AM sometimes. Not always from Alex's or Evan's nightmares. Sometimes from my own. But now, instead of wrestling with the ceiling, I whisper what Aunt Gee taught me: "Jesus, be near."

And somehow, in the darkness, He always is.

CHAPTER FIVE

Faith Together

How Spiritual Community Builds Resilience

The divorce papers sat on my kitchen counter like a live grenade with the pin pulled. Wednesday night in Miami, late 2007, the humidity was so thick you could swim through it. I was sitting in my SUV outside Fellowship church, engine running, AC blasting, dashboard clock glowing 7:18 PM. Men's group started at 7:30. Twelve minutes to decide whether to drive away or walk in.

My 2002 Mazda Tribute, dark blue with a dent in the passenger door from when Elizabeth backed into it with her new 2006 Mazda RX-8. The AC was making that clicking noise it did when the compressor was dying, would cost $800 to fix according to the guy at Midas. I had $247 in my checking account. The divorce lawyer wanted $3,500 just to start. Math wasn't adding up anywhere in my life.

The parking lot was half-full. Could see other guys walking toward the portable building, that's what Fellowship called their overflow space, basically a double-wide trailer they'd bought from a construction company. Tan metal siding, three window units struggling against Miami humidity, carpet that smelled like mildew no matter how much Febreze they sprayed.

My hands wouldn't stop shaking. Not from the coffee I'd mainlined all day to stay functional. Not from the humidity that made everything feel like you were breathing through a wet towel. From the knowledge

99

that my marriage was over, that I'd failed again, that the God I'd tried so hard to serve seemed to specialize in letting me crash and burn.

The papers came from a polished law firm in Coral Gables. Elizabeth had hired them. Eighty pages of legal language that might as well have said, "You failed. Again. Here's how we'll divide the wreckage."

Page thirty-seven listed what we'd built, and what was left of it.

A 2002 Mazda Tribute that still smelled like motor oil and fast food.

Her 2006 Mazda RX-8 that always started, even when we didn't.

A checking account with $1,247.

Savings: zero.

Retirement: barely eighteen thousand.

Debt: forty-seven grand.

Seven years of shared dreams, laughter, and silence, summed up on paper.

A marriage reduced to numbers that couldn't capture the love that once tried to live between them.

The stack of papers on my passenger seat might as well have been a neon sign flashing "FAILURE" in red letters. This was supposed to be different. The LDS church was supposed to provide structure. The temple marriage was supposed to be eternal. The strict guidelines were supposed to keep us on track. But here I was, thirty-five years old, about to be divorced, sitting outside a church I'd only been attending for six months because I couldn't face the LDS ward where everyone knew my business.

Then Mike knocked on my window.

Made me jump so hard I spilled coffee on my lap. Gas station coffee, $1.29 from the RaceTrac on Coral Reef Drive. Now I had divorce papers AND a coffee stain on my khakis. Perfect.

Mike...Samson, we called him. Six-foot-four electrician with hands like catcher's mitts and a heart even bigger. Covered in tattoos from a past he rarely discussed, but his eyes held a kindness that made you want to trust him with your worst secrets. He had this way of tilting his head when he looked at you, like he could see past whatever mask you were wearing.

"You coming in, brother?"

He was wearing a faded Dolphins jersey, Dan Marino, number 13. Later, I found out it was his lucky shirt. Wore it to every men's group for three years until his wife threw it away because it had more holes than fabric. The man cried actual tears over that jersey.

That word, brother. Not friend. Not buddy. Not even "man" or "dude." Brother. Like we were family. Like I belonged. Like showing up with divorce papers in my truck and failure in my pocket didn't disqualify me from being part of something.

I wanted to tell him everything. About the papers. About how I'd already failed at this once before. About how my faith felt like tissue paper in a hurricane, dissolving the moment real pressure hit. Instead, I just nodded and killed the engine.

The walk from my truck to the portable building was maybe fifty yards. Felt like a mile. Could hear the window units struggling, dripping condensation like they were sweating too. Someone had put a handwritten sign on the door: "Men's Group, Enter at Your Own Risk." Below that, someone else had written in Sharpie: "Seriously, we're all messed up in here."

Truth in advertising.

The Weight of Going It Alone

That night changed everything, but let me back up and tell you how I got there. How I learned the hard way that isolation isn't strength, it's slow-motion suicide.

I learned about isolation in Kowloon. 2012, fresh off divorce number two, living in a 600-square-foot apartment that cost more than most American mortgages. The walls were so thin I could hear my neighbor's alarm clock. The kitchen was so small I could touch both walls with my arms spread. The bed was a futon on the floor because committing to actual furniture felt too permanent, too much like admitting this was my life now.

Willow Mansions, Whampoa Garden, Unit 2707. 18,000 HKD a month, about $2,300 US. For that price in Texas, I could've rented a mansion. In Hong Kong, I got a glorified closet with a view of another building's laundry. My neighbor to the left was learning violin, badly. My neighbor to the right had a parrot that screamed Cantonese obscenities at 6 AM. The couple upstairs had vigorous relations every Thursday at 11 PM. You could set your watch by it.

My routine was robotic: Wake at 4 AM to the sound of the first MTR trains. Work until 10 PM because the office was better than the empty apartment. Grab noodles from 7-Eleven—always the XO sauce seafood flavor—for $18 HKD. Add a tall can of San Miguel, $12 HKD, cold enough to sweat in the humid neon night. Fall asleep to TVB variety shows I couldn't understand, the canned laughter a mockery of my loneliness.

I had exactly three DVDs I'd bought from the lady selling bootlegs in Mong Kok: The Shawshank Redemption, Gladiator, and inexplicably, Bridget Jones's Diary. Watched them on repeat on my laptop. Can still quote Maximus's speech about vengeance in the afterlife. "Father to a murdered son, husband to a murdered wife, and I will have my vengeance, in this life or the next." Felt appropriate for a man whose life had been murdered by his own choices.

I had my Bible app, YouVersion, downloaded in seventeen languages like that would somehow make God's voice clearer. Had my prayer journal that was mostly empty pages because writing "help" over and over felt redundant. Even watched Andy Stanley sermons on my laptop, telling myself that virtual church was still church. See? Totally fine.

Except I wasn't.

One Tuesday morning, March 13, 2012, 6:47 AM according to my journal, I woke up with this crushing weight on my chest. Couldn't breathe right. Heart racing like I'd run a marathon in my sleep. The room was spinning even though I was lying still. Thought I was having a heart attack. Called a taxi to take me to the hospital, certain I was dying at forty in a country where I couldn't even properly explain my symptoms.

The taxi driver, an old Chinese guy who smelled like cigarettes and Tiger Balm, kept looking at me in the rearview mirror. "You okay, mister? You okay?" I wanted to say no, I'm dying, but all I could manage was pointing at my chest and gasping like a fish out of water. The ride to Queen Elizabeth Hospital cost $127 HKD. Longest fifteen minutes of my life.

The ER doctor, a young woman who looked about twelve, ran an EKG, blood tests, and a chest X-ray. Everything normal. "Panic attack," she said in perfect British-accented English. "Very common with expats. Isolation, stress, cultural adjustment." She prescribed Xanax and told me to "find community."

Find community. Like it was something you could order on Amazon.

Turned out to be a panic attack. My body's way of screaming what my soul already knew: humans aren't designed to do life alone. We're not wired for isolation. Even God, who needs nothing and no one, exists in community, Father, Son, Holy Spirit. And here I was, trying to survive solo, wondering why I was falling apart.

Why We Hide (And Why We Shouldn't)

Let me get real with you. Growing up in La Porte, Texas, in a blue-collar family where my dad was an electrician and my mom worked as a beautician, I learned early that men handle their own problems. My dad was the kind of guy who fixed everything himself: cars, appliances, plumbing, you name it. When my parents' marriage began to crack, he didn't go to counseling. He just buried himself in work. When it finally shattered, he kept the house, paid her off—like settling a debt—and stayed. The walls absorbed his silence, the rooms echoing with absence. He mowed the lawn, patched the roof, and pretended the house wasn't haunted by everything it had lost.

Dad's toolbox, Craftsman, red metal, bought in 1973, had everything except tools for fixing a broken heart. I found it after he died, still organized perfectly. Screwdrivers by size. Wrenches in order. A place for everything and everything in its place. Except there was no place for the bottle of Jack Daniel's hidden behind the socket set. No slot for the antidepressants he never told anyone he was taking. No drawer for the letter from Mom he'd kept for twenty years, still in its envelope, never opened.

That's the masculinity I inherited: competent with everything except emotions. Could rebuild an engine but couldn't rebuild a relationship. Could wire a house but couldn't connect with another human being.

That's the model I inherited. Handle your business. Don't burden others. Definitely don't cry in front of people. Real men carry their own weight, even when that weight is crushing them.

But that night in Miami, sitting in that circle of mismatched chairs in the church's portable building, it wasn't even a real building, just a double-wide trailer they'd converted, I discovered something revolutionary: every man in that circle was carrying invisible weight.

The chairs were donations from various places. Two brown folding chairs from a funeral home. Three plastic ones from someone's patio set. A rolling office chair with one broken wheel. A wooden stool that looked like it came from a bar. We sat in a circle because, as Mike said, "Nobody gets to hide in the back row when there is no back row."

The portable itself was a masterclass in making do. Wood paneling from the '80s. Carpet tiles that didn't quite match, some gray, some blue, one random red one, like someone ran out and said, "close enough." A coffee maker from 1987 that made sounds like it was dying but somehow produced the strongest, most necessary coffee in Miami.

Jim's shame had a number: $280,000 in debt from a business venture that went sideways. He'd been hiding bills in his garage, lying to his wife about their finances, considering driving his car off the Rickenbacker Causeway because the life insurance would take care of his family.

Jim drove a 2007 Lexus LS 460. Leather seats. Navigation system. $78,000 car that he couldn't afford to put gas in. He'd park it two blocks away and walk to the men's group so nobody would see him putting $5 of gas in a luxury car. Pride and poverty make terrible roommates.

Carlos's fear had a name: his son Michael, seventeen years old, honor student turned heroin addict. Carlos had found needles in Michael's backpack, confronted him, and Michael had disappeared for three days. When he came back, he was high and hostile, and Carlos, a tough Miami contractor who'd built half the condos on Brickell, had cried like a baby.

Carlos showed us a photo that night. Michael, in his National Honor Society polo shirt, holding his acceptance letter to the University of Florida. Full scholarship. Engineering program. The photo was from eight months earlier. Carlos said Michael now weighed ninety pounds less and had been arrested twice. Same kid, different universe. Heroin is a time machine that only goes backward.

Tom's grief had a timeline: six months, the doctors said. His wife, Sarah, had stage 4 pancreatic cancer. They'd been married thirty-seven years, high school sweethearts, never spent more than two nights apart. Now he was practicing being alone, and every practice session felt like drowning.

Tom brought Sarah's scarf to the meeting. Silk, with little butterflies on it. Said it still smelled like her perfume, White Shoulders, the same kind she'd worn since high school. He'd wrap it around his hands while he talked, like he was holding onto her by a thread. Which, I guess, he was.

And my guilt? It had a specific geography. An island. A highway. A moment in the Caribbean that changed everything. Plus, two failed marriages that felt like evidence God had given up on me.

The apostle Paul understood this: "Carry each other's burdens, and in this way you will fulfill the law of Christ" (Galatians 6:2, NIV). Notice he didn't say "Fix each other's burdens," or "Judge each other's burdens," or "Give advice about each other's burdens." Just carry. Just be present. Just acknowledge that none of us are meant to do this alone.

That first night, nobody tried to fix me. Nobody quoted Romans 8:28 at me like a biblical band-aid. Mike just said, "Divorce sucks, brother. My first one nearly killed me." Jim said, "Failed marriages feel like failed faith, don't they?" Carlos just nodded; his English wasn't excellent when emotion was involved. Tom reached over and put his hand on my shoulder. Didn't say anything. Didn't need to. His hand shook a little, probably thinking about practicing being alone, but he held it there anyway.

That's when I started crying. Not pretty tears. Ugly crying. Snot and everything. In a room full of men, I'd known for six months. In a portable building that smelled like mildew and burnt coffee. In Miami heat that made everything feel like you were drowning in air.

And nobody looked away. Nobody got uncomfortable. Nobody tried to stop me.

They just let me break. Because they'd all broken too. And they knew that sometimes breaking is the only way to let the light in.

The Unexpected Power of Showing Up

After that first night in Miami, I almost didn't go back. Pride is a funny thing; it'll convince you that you're protecting others from your mess when really, you're just protecting yourself from being known. It whispers lies like "They don't really want you there," "You're too broken for community," and "Real men don't need support groups."

Spent the whole week making excuses. Wednesday came around again. I was sitting in the same truck, in the same parking lot, at 7:18 PM again. Like Groundhog Day for damaged Christians. This time, I had a list of reasons not to go in:

1. The Cowboys were playing (they weren't)

2. Needed to work late (I was already in the parking lot)

3. Coming down with something (unless cowardice is contagious, I was fine)

4. They probably didn't even notice I was there last week (lie)

My phone buzzed at 7:19. Text from Mike, just three words: "See you inside?"

Not "See you Wednesday?" like I could skip it. "See you inside?" like he was already counting on me being there. Like my empty chair would matter.

No pressure. No preaching. Just an invitation to show up.

I went back. And something strange started happening. The more I showed up, the lighter the weight became. Not because my circumstances changed, the divorce still went through, the guilt from the Caribbean still haunted me, the questions about God's plan still swirled. But because I wasn't carrying it alone anymore.

Week three, Jim brought donuts. Not fancy donuts. Day-old from Publix, $3.99 for a dozen. But he got them because "men need sugar to talk about feelings." He was right. Something about powdered sugar on your fingers makes vulnerability less terrifying.

Week five, Carlos taught us to curse in Spanish. Not proud of it, but when he was talking about finding needles in Michael's room, English failed him. The Spanish profanity that followed needed no translation. We all felt it. Sometimes holy anger sounds like unholy words.

Week eight, Tom didn't come. Sarah was in hospice. We went to him instead. Eight grown men standing in his living room, not knowing what to say, so we just stood there. Mike finally said, "We're here to help you practice not being alone." Tom broke down. We all did. Sarah died two days later. We were pallbearers. Carried her casket and Tom's grief in equal measure.

There's this moment I'll never forget. Maybe six months into the group, Jim was sharing about a business opportunity that felt too good to be true. After the bankruptcy, he was gun-shy about everything, second-guessing every decision, paralyzed by the fear of failing again.

The opportunity was buying into a food truck franchise. Initial investment: $45,000. Jim had $8,000 from selling his Lexus and driving a 1997 Toyota Corolla with 230,000 miles and a driver's door that wouldn't open from the inside. Had to roll down the window and open it from outside like he was in a bad comedy sketch.

"I can't tell if this is God opening a door or Satan dressed up like opportunity," Jim said.

We spent two hours reviewing the business plan. Mike knew construction costs. Carlos knew permits; half of success in Miami is knowing whose palm to grease. I knew contracts from my consulting work. Tom knew nothing about business, but knew Jim needed us to take this seriously.

When Jim finished, Eduardo, a quiet guy who barely said two words most nights, worked construction, hands permanently stained with concrete dust, cleared his throat.

Eduardo's English was learned on job sites. He knew every construction term but struggled with regular conversation. His prayers were half English, half Spanish, all heart.

"I know a guy," Eduardo said in accented English. "Used to work with him in construction. Owns three food trucks now. Straight shooter. Good man. I'll make a call."

That introduction led Jim to rebuild his contracting business. But here's what mattered more: Eduardo saw Jim. Not the bankruptcy. Not the failure. Not the guy who'd considered suicide. He saw Jim the man, Jim the father, Jim the child of God who deserved another chance.

Jim's food truck, "Jim's Genuine BBQ," opened eight months later. We all worked the first day for free. Mike nearly burned down the truck trying to work the grill. Carlos refused to take off his Miami Heat jersey even though the health code required an apron. Tom kept giving away free food to pretty women because "Sarah would want me to be generous." Eduardo just smiled and kept saying "Is good, is good" to every customer.

Made $1,247 that first day. Jim cried when he counted it. Same amount that had been in his checking account when his first business failed.

That's what real spiritual community does. It sees past the wreckage to the person God's still working on.

When Church Feels Like Sandpaper

Frankly speaking, sometimes church is the last place you want to be. I remember sitting in a Sunday service in 2014, two years after my second divorce, listening to a sermon series on "Building Strong Marriages." Every week for six weeks. It felt like God was using a cheese grater on my soul.

Pastor Richards. Good man, terrible timing. Had been married to his high school sweetheart for thirty-two years. Three kids, all in ministry. His biggest marital crisis was arguing about what color to paint the bathroom. He'd stand up there with his perfect family photos on the screen behind him, everyone in matching white shirts on a beach, of course, talking about "God's design for marriage."

Week three was "Divorce-Proofing Your Marriage." I wanted to stand up and yell, "A bit late for that, Pastor!" Instead, I sat there calculating how many ceiling tiles were in the sanctuary. 247. I counted three times.

The pastor, well-meaning guy with a perfect family and probably perfect credit score, said something about how "God hates divorce," quoting Malachi 2:16. I knew he was quoting scripture, but in that moment, all I heard was "God hates you."

I was halfway out of my pew, ready to never come back, when this elderly woman named Dorothy grabbed my arm. She had those paper-thin hands that shook a little with age, skin like parchment, blue veins showing through, but her grip was surprisingly firm.

Dorothy. Four-foot-eleven in heels. Wore the same purple dress every Sunday with different brooches. Had been at that church since 1962. Sat in the same spot, third row, left side, aisle seat, for fifty-two years. The one time someone accidentally sat in her spot, she stood next to them until they moved. Nobody messed with Dorothy's spot after that.

"Sit with me," she said. Not a question. A gentle command.

After the service, while everyone else was rushing to beat the lunch crowd, she told me about her son, three divorces, two kids he rarely saw, and a grandson he'd never met because his ex-wife had moved to California.

She pulled out her phone—a flip phone from 2003—and showed me a photo she'd taken of a photo. Her son, Robert. Looked just like her, with the same determined jaw and the same eyes that had seen too much. "He's fifty-seven now," she said. "Still thinks God's given up on him. I tell him God doesn't give up, but people get tired of waiting for Him to show up."

"I pray for him every day," she said, her voice steady but her eyes wet. "And now I'll pray for you too. Not for God to fix your situation, that's already done. But for you to feel His love in the middle of your mess."

She did pray for me. Every day for the next year, until she passed away. I know because she'd send me these little cards, the kind you buy at the dollar store, nothing fancy, with Bible verses written in shaky handwriting. Still have them in a shoebox.

Thirty-seven cards total. Dollar Tree cards with puppies, kittens, flowers, and one random Halloween card she sent in July with "God loves you" written where it should say "Trick or Treat." My favorite: a birthday card (not my birthday) that said "Another Year Older" on the front. Inside, she'd written: "Another day God's not done with you yet. -D"

Dorothy died on a Tuesday. Found out when her purple dress spot was empty on Sunday. Pastor Richards announced it during prayer requests. Said she'd died in her sleep, Bible open to Psalm 91, pen in her hand, my name on a prayer list on her nightstand.

Whenever I doubt that God cares, I pull out those cards and remember Dorothy, who barely knew me but loved me anyway.

Building Your Spiritual Support System

So how do you actually build this kind of community? Because let's be honest, walking into a church when your life's a mess feels about as comfortable as a root canal without anesthesia.

Start small. You don't need a crowd. Jesus said, "Where two or three gather in my name, there am I with them" (Matthew 18:20, NIV). Two or three. That's it. That's church.

My smallest "church" was me and a guy named Frank at a Waffle House in Huntsville, Alabama. Both traveling for work. Both eating alone at 11 PM. Started talking about football, ended talking about faith. Met there every time we were both in town, maybe four times total. Frank died of COVID in 2020. His wife sent me a message on Facebook: "You're the Waffle House friend? Frank said you helped him believe again."

Two people. Scattered eggs and scattered faith. That's church.

When Stefaniya and I moved back to Texas in 2016, we visited twelve churches. Twelve! Some had smoke machines and light shows that belonged in Vegas. Others had organs older than Moses and hymns that sounded like funeral dirges. One had a pastor who yelled so much I wondered if he thought God was deaf. Another had a pastor who whispered, as if he were afraid of waking God up.

Church #3: Fog machine triggered the fire alarm. Entire congregation evacuated during "How Great Is Our God." Church #7: Pastor's toupee shifted during baptism. Nobody said anything. Most uncomfortable thirty minutes of my life. Church #9: Communion

113

wine was definitely Welch's grape juice mixed with something else. Maybe Sprite? Church #11: Children's choir sang "This Little Light of Mine" so off-key that a baby started crying and wouldn't stop. Baby had the right idea.

We weren't looking for perfect production or polished performances. We were looking for broken people who knew they were broken and weren't pretending otherwise.

Give it time. Real relationships aren't microwaveable. They're more like smoking a brisket, low and slow, can't rush the process, and the result is worth the wait.

It took me three years to break into that Slavic community in Hong Kong. Three years of showing up to services where I understood maybe every tenth word. Three years of drinking tea I didn't like (who puts jam in tea?) and eating food I couldn't identify. Three years of smiling and nodding when I had no idea what was happening.

The food. Lord, help me. Holodets, meat jelly. Looks like someone suspended hot dogs in Jell-O. Tastes worse than it looks. Olivier salad, potatoes, eggs, pickles, and enough mayonnaise to caulk a bathtub. Herring under a fur coat, layers of fish, beets, and more mayonnaise. Many Ukrainians and Russians really love mayonnaise.

But I ate it all. Every Sunday. With a smile. Because community sometimes tastes like things you'd never order but eat anyway because love is on the menu.

But those relationships? They're the reason I met Stefaniya. They're the reason I learned that faith transcends language. They're the reason I discovered that sometimes the best community is the one where you don't fit, but they make room for you anyway.

Serve somewhere. Nothing builds bonds faster than working alongside people. When Stefaniya and I started serving in children's ministry, mainly because they were desperate and we were available, we discovered something beautiful. Kids don't care about your past. They don't care that you've been divorced. They don't care that you carry guilt from decades ago. They just want someone to listen to their Bible story presentation and tell them they did a great job.

Teaching four-year-olds is like herding cats who've had espresso. Last month, little Timmy asked, "Mr. Simon, why did Jesus have to die?" Before I could answer with something theologically sound, Susie piped up: "Because the bad guys were mean and God said no more!" Timmy nodded, as if this made perfect sense. Sometimes four-year-old theology is the best theology.

One kid, Marcus, always wants to play David and Goliath. He's three feet tall and insists on being Goliath. Falls dramatically every time. Oscar-worthy performances. His Goliath always says, "Ow, that really hurt!" before dying. Biblical accuracy is questionable. Heart is in the right place.

There's something healing about serving others when you're broken. It reminds you that God doesn't wait until we're whole to use us. He uses broken people to help other broken people, and somehow, in the process, we all get a little less broken.

The Multiplication Effect

Here's what blows my mind about spiritual community: it multiplies. Remember Jim from that Miami men's group? The guy with the bankruptcy, Eduardo, helped. He now runs a ministry for men going through financial crisis. Meets every Saturday morning at a

Denny's off Biscayne Boulevard. Last count, forty guys show up regularly. Forty! From one introduction, one act of seeing someone beyond their failure.

Jim's ministry is called "Broke But Not Broken." They have t-shirts. Comic Sans font because Jim has no design sense, but a huge heart. The back says, "Ask Me About My Debt," which is either terrible or genius. Maybe both.

They meet at Denny's, where the hostess, Carmen, saves them a table in the back room. She lost her house in 2008 and knows what financial ruin feels like. Always "forgets" to charge for coffee refills. God's economy involves free coffee when you're broke.

Carlos? His son got clean. It wasn't quick or easy. There were relapses, arrests, and overdoses that should have killed him. But Carlos never gave up, and neither did that men's group. We prayed for Michael every week for three years.

Michael's sobriety date: October 7, 2010. Has it tattooed on his wrist where track marks used to be. Goes to NA meetings in the same church portable where we had men's group. Circle of redemption. He sponsors three guys now. One just celebrated five years clean. Mathematics of recovery: one saves three, three save nine, nine save twenty-seven. Exponential grace.

Now Carlos and Michael run recovery meetings together at their church. Carlos shares the parents' perspective, Michael shares the addict's perspective, and together they offer hope that families can survive addiction.

Tom? His wife, Sarah, died eight months after that first meeting I attended. We all went to the funeral. Sat together in the back row, a bunch of broken men trying to hold each other up. Tom thought his life was over. But the group wouldn't let him disappear.

Tom's disappearing act was professional-level. Wouldn't answer texts. Changed his locks. Once, Mike climbed through Tom's bathroom window to check on him. Found Tom sitting in Sarah's closet, surrounded by her clothes, holding that butterfly scarf. Mike just sat down next to him. Didn't say anything. Just sat there in a dead woman's closet with a grieving man. That's brotherhood.

Two years later, Tom met Patricia, a widow from our church. They got married last spring. Tom says he never thought he'd love again, but God had other plans.

Tom and Patricia's wedding was in the portable building. Her idea. Said fancy churches were for first marriages; second chances deserve honest venues. Mike was the best man. Cried through the entire ceremony. Eduardo's daughter sang in Spanish; nobody understood the words, but everybody understood the feeling. Jim catered with his food truck. Free BBQ is a love language for broken men who have found brotherhood.

The Sacred Secret of Shared Weakness

Paul says something profound in 2 Corinthians: "Praise be to the God and Father of our Lord Jesus Christ, the Father of compassion and the God of all comfort, who comforts us in all our troubles, so that we can comfort those in any trouble with the comfort we ourselves receive from God" (2 Corinthians 1:3-4, NIV).

Do you see it? The comfort we receive was never meant to stop with us. It becomes the comfort we give. Our pain, once shared in community, becomes someone else's lifeline. It's spiritual math that makes no sense: broken plus broken doesn't equal more broken. It equals healing.

Last month, a new guy showed up at our men's group. Derek. Twenty-eight years old. Wife just left. Took the kids. He sat there shaking like I did that first night in Miami. Couldn't even say his name without crying.

Mike looked at him and said, "Brother, every man in this circle has been where you are." Then we went around the circle. Every man shared his worst moment. Not his testimony with the shiny ending. His worst moment.

When it got to me, I said, "I've killed someone. Been divorced twice. Failed at everything that matters." Derek looked at me like I was speaking Mandarin. Then he said, "And you're still here?"

"Still here," I said. "So are you. That's all God needs, us still being here."

YOUR NEXT STEP

This week, reach out to one person and share something real. Not your highlight reel. Not your testimony with all the rough edges sanded off. Something you're actually struggling with right now.

If you're thinking "I don't have anyone," here's your starter list:

• The guy who sits alone at church (he's there every week, third row from the back, left side)

• The woman who tears up during worship (she's fighting something)

• The teenager who looks angry (they're drowning)

• The elderly person who sits in the same spot (they've got stories)

• The new person who looks lost (they are)

Text someone right now. Not later. Now. Three words: "Can we talk?" or "Need your prayers" or my personal favorite: "Life's hard today."

Find your people. The broken ones. The honest ones. The ones who'll knock on your window when you're about to drive away.

Community doesn't always look like what we expect. Sometimes it's a text at 2 AM. Sometimes it's sitting in silence with someone who's grieving. Sometimes it's showing up at someone's house with pizza and no agenda except to be present.

My community includes:

• Mike, who still texts me every Month: "See you tonight?" even though I moved to Texas

• James from the Singapore airport, who emails me every Christmas

• Mr. Chen from the ramen shop, who doesn't speak English but somehow said everything

• Dorothy's cards in a shoebox

• Three men in Dallas who meet me for coffee and never let me get away with BS

• Stefaniya, who knows all my worst parts and chooses to stay anyway

Find your people. It'll change everything. Not because they'll fix you, they won't. But because they'll sit with you in the portable building of life, with its mismatched chairs and terrible coffee and mildew smell, and remind you that broken together is better than perfect alone.

That's church. That's community. That's the Gospel with skin on it.

CHAPTER SIX

Anchored in the Word

Timeless Scriptures That Sustain Us in Crisis

The rain hammered against my office window that Tuesday morning like an angry creditor demanding payment. Each drop seemed to echo the emails piling up in my inbox, the calls I wasn't returning, the reality I was avoiding. I sat in my home office, which sounds impressive until you realize it's just a converted bedroom pretending to be important, laptop closed, watching the storm roll in from the west. The weather app said it would pass by noon. The storm in my business wouldn't pass nearly as quickly.

October 17, 2023. 8:34 AM. I know because I screenshot my phone when things feel significant, like maybe I'll need evidence later that this moment actually happened. The screenshot shows 53 unread emails, four missed calls, and a text from my accountant that said, "Call me." When your accountant texts instead of emailing, you're in trouble.

The office wasn't really an office. It started as our youngest daughter's nursery, but when COVID hit and everyone pretended working from home was temporary, it slowly turned into "Daddy's work room." Sherwin-Williams "Agreeable Gray" on the walls—Stefaniya's choice. She said it was calming. Right now, it felt more like being inside a storm cloud.

Fifty-three unread emails blinked at me from my phone screen, each one a small red accusation. I knew what they contained without opening them. After thirty years of building businesses across continents, I recognized the death rattle of a failing enterprise. The careful language of vendors wanting payment. The increasingly urgent subject lines from investors. The polite-but-firm reminders from the bank.

My coffee had gone cold an hour ago. Steam long vanished, like my confidence, my plans, my sense that I had any control over anything. Outside, a lone mockingbird, our Texas state bird, huddled under the eaves of my neighbor's house, riding out the storm with more dignity than I was managing. The sight triggered something profound, a memory of Scripture from decades ago: "Are not two sparrows sold for a penny? Yet not one of them will fall to the ground outside your Father's care" (Matthew 10:29, NIV).

The neighbor's house is Jim and Linda Patterson's, who are retired teachers who moved here from Ohio. They keep bird feeders that attract every mockingbird in a five-mile radius. Jim told me once that mockingbirds can learn up to 200 different songs. "They're basically the cover bands of the bird world," he said. That morning, watching one huddle against the storm, I wondered what song it would sing when the rain stopped. If it would sing at all.

Funny how Scripture hits different when you're the one falling.

When Everything Falls Apart (And God Feels Silent)

I thought back to my father's stories, told over lukewarm Folgers coffee in our La Porte kitchen when I was maybe eight or nine. He'd work double shifts at the plant, come home exhausted, but somehow find energy to tell me about David and Goliath, about Daniel in the lion's den, about Paul in prison. His voice would crack sometimes when he'd talk about Job's losses. I think he saw himself in that story, a good man trying to understand why life kept dealing him bad hands.

Dad worked at a chemical plant in Freeport. Forty-minute drive each way. Left at 5 AM, home by 6 PM if he wasn't pulling overtime. His hands were permanently stained with whatever chemicals they used, looking like faint blue ink under his skin. He'd sit at our Aqua blue with gold specks Formica table, still in his work clothes that smelled like sulfur and exhaustion, drinking coffee from a mug that said "World's Greatest Dad" in letters that were half worn off.

"You know what Job said?" he'd ask, though I never did. I was eight. I thought Job was somebody he worked with.

"He said, 'The Lord gives and the Lord takes away. Blessed be the name of the Lord.'" Dad would pause, stare into his coffee like it held answers. "That's faith, son. Blessing God when He's taking away."

I'd nod like I understood. I didn't. Not until October 17, 2023, sitting in my gray office, watching everything I'd built wash away in a Texas thunderstorm.

Back then, sitting at that Formica table with my legs swinging because they couldn't reach the floor, those felt like adventure stories—heroes of faith who always came out on top. Now, at fifty-three, watching my business empire crumble faster than I could rebuild it, they felt like the only lifeline in rough seas.

The old house creaked in the storm. Texas humidity does that to wood frames, makes everything swell and contract, like the house is breathing. Or sighing. Everything felt tired. The spreadsheets I'd created in Singapore, revised in Dubai, and polished in Hong Kong, all showing projections that would never materialize. The five-year plan

I'd presented to investors with such confidence. The carefully crafted business model that didn't account for pandemics, supply chain disruptions, or the simple fact that sometimes, despite your best efforts, things fall apart.

The five-year plan was beautiful. Sixty-seven slides. Professional graphics I'd paid a designer in Austin $3,500 to create. Revenue projections that went up and to the right like they're supposed to. Year one: $2.3 million. Year five: $18.7 million. I'd presented it in the conference room at Capital Factory downtown, wearing my lucky tie, the blue one with tiny elephants that Stefaniya bought me for our anniversary.

The investors nodded at all the right places. Asked smart questions. One guy, a venture capitalist from Dallas with a Tesla in every color, said it was "the most thorough deck he'd seen all year."

That was January 2023. By October, we'd burned through $800,000 with nothing to show but a product nobody wanted and a team of twelve people I couldn't afford to pay.

No one really prepares you for what faith feels like when life falls apart; it's not pretty. It's not Instagram-worthy with perfectly highlighted Bible verses and artfully arranged coffee cups. It's sitting in yesterday's t-shirt at 3 AM, wondering if those ancient words written for shepherds and fishermen have any bearing on your modern disaster. It's opening your Bible app because your actual Bible is buried somewhere in the garage, and even finding it feels like too much effort.

The Stories That Save Us

I sit in my study with my beat-up NIV Bible before the kids wake up. They always catch me, no matter how quiet I try to be. But right now, before Stefaniya starts making breakfast with that efficiency that still amazes me, it's just me and scripture in the quiet. The one I bought in Miami back in 2003, when I thought joining a new church would fix everything. Coffee in one hand, pen in the other. I don't just read; I wrestle.

The Bible's held together with duct tape now. Silver duct tape because that's what was in the garage. Genesis is missing pages 1-15. Revelations' last page is gone. It's like my faith, missing the beginning and the end, holding onto the middle for dear life.

My morning routine: 4:47 AM alarm. Don't ask why 4:47; it just feels less aggressive than 4:45. French press coffee: 18 grams of beans to 300 grams of water. Yes, I weigh my coffee. Control what you can when everything else is chaos. Sit in the leather chair I bought at an estate sale for $50. The previous owner died in it, according to the seller. Didn't bother me. We're all dying in something.

Take Job, for instance. Here's a guy who lost everything: wealth, family, health. His wife told him to curse God and die. His friends told him he must have sinned. His body was covered in boils that he scraped with broken pottery, the ancient equivalent of self-harm, really. I used to skip to the end where he got everything back, doubled even. These days, I camp out in the middle chapters where he's arguing with God, demanding answers, getting cosmic silence in response.

Job 13:15 in my Bible is underlined so many times the page is worn through: "Though he slay me, yet will I hope in him; I will surely defend my ways to his face."

Next to it, I've written in different inks from different years:

- 2003: "I don't understand this"

- 2007: "Still don't get it"

- 2012: "Maybe starting to understand"

- 2015: "This is insane faith"

- 2023: "This is the only kind of faith that survives"

That's not blind faith. That's defiant trust. That's saying, "I don't understand You, I'm angry at You, but I'm not letting go of You." That's faith with clenched fists.

Or consider Paul. The guy wrote Philippians from a Roman prison. Not a county jail with visiting hours and commissary privileges. We're talking about house arrest with guards, chains, and the constant possibility of execution. Yet he writes, "I have learned the secret of being content in any and every situation" (Philippians 4:12, NIV).

I threw my Bible once after reading that. Actually threw it. Hit the wall in my Hong Kong apartment, leaving a dent. The pages fluttered down like wounded birds, landing somewhere in Romans. The neighbor banged back. I stood there, hand still extended, staring at the dent like I'd just punched God himself. I wanted to yell through the wall, "It's the apostle Paul's fault."

Content? In prison? Content with chains digging into his wrists, while Rome decided whether to kill him? Content with everything God promised falling apart?

Then it hit me. Four words that changed everything: 'I have learned.'

Not 'I am naturally.' Not 'God made me,' but 'I have learned.' Like contentment was a foreign language, Paul had to study while bleeding. Which means there was a before. A Paul who raged at God. A Paul who probably punched walls in Damascus after going blind. A Paul who lay awake counting all the ways this wasn't what he'd signed up for when

Jesus knocked him off his horse.

Paul had to learn contentment the same way I learned to live with guilt—one impossible day at a time.

Making Ancient Words Modern

Here's what I've discovered traveling from Hong Kong boardrooms to Jerusalem's Western Wall: human nature hasn't upgraded. We've got smartphones instead of scrolls, email instead of epistles, but we're asking the same questions. Why is this happening? Where is God? Will I make it through? How long, O Lord, how long?

Standing at the Western Wall in 2005, I watched an Orthodox Jewish man davening, that rocking prayer motion, with such intensity I thought he might go through the stones. He was holding a smartphone in one hand, a prayer book in the other. Ancient words, modern problems. When he finished, he kissed the wall and checked his messages immediately. That's all of us, one foot in eternity, one in the urgent now.

The Psalms are basically the world's oldest blog. David processing his emotions in real-time, not cleaning them up for public consumption. "My God, my God, why have you forsaken me?" (Psalm 22:1, NIV). Jesus quoted that on the cross, which means even the Son of God felt abandoned. If Jesus can feel forsaken and still be perfect, maybe my feelings of abandonment don't disqualify me from faith.

Psalm 22 in my Bible has a coffee ring on it. Spilled an entire cup during a particularly aggressive wrestling match with verse 1. The stain makes the words look like they're dissolving, which feels appropriate. Sometimes faith dissolves before it resolidifies.

David wrote that psalm while running from Saul. Sleeping in caves.

Eating whatever he could scavenge. The future king of Israel, already anointed, was hiding like a criminal. I wonder if he thought Samuel got the wrong guy. "Maybe the oil was meant for my brother. Maybe God changed His mind."

My SCRIPT Method (Because I Need Systems)

After years in the tech industry, I've come to appreciate frameworks. Systems. Processes. Something to follow when my emotions are too chaotic to trust. So, I developed this approach to Scripture during a crisis. Call it SCRIPT:

I actually wrote this on a whiteboard in my office first. Dry erase markers in different colors because my brain needs visual organization. Stefaniya walked in while I was mapping it out, connecting verses with arrows like I was solving a crime.

"What are you doing?" she asked.

"Systematizing faith," I said.

"Only you would make a spreadsheet for God," she laughed. But she wasn't wrong.

S - Situate the Context: I learned this from a pastor in Ephesus, of all places. Standing where Paul preached, in the ruins of the ancient library, he said, "You can't understand the message without understanding the messenger's world."

That pastor, Williams—I think that was his name—from Dallas Theological Seminary led a study tour I joined in 2011. Forty-two hundred dollars for ten days, airfare not included. Standing in the Library of Celsus, 102°F in the shade (and there was no shade), sweat ran down my back like my own body was baptizing me as he told us to close our eyes.

"Imagine Paul here. No air conditioning. No amplification. Competing with merchants, prostitutes from the temple of Artemis, and Roman soldiers keeping order. Now read Ephesians."

Suddenly, "Put on the full armor of God" wasn't metaphorical. Paul could see Roman soldiers while writing it. Their armor was what kept them alive. Paul was saying, "You need protection too, but not from swords, from something worse."

So, when I read Paul's prison letters, I picture house arrest. Not metaphorical chains, real ones. Guards who probably smelled like garlic and sweat. The constant clanking of metal. The humiliation of needing permission for everything. Suddenly, "rejoice always" isn't a happy platitude; it's an act of rebellion against circumstances.

When I read David's psalms, I remember he wrote many of them while running from Saul, sleeping in caves, wondering if each day would be his last. "The LORD is my light and my salvation, whom shall I fear?" (Psalm 27:1, NIV) hits different when you know it was written by a man with a price on his head.

C - Connect to Current Reality: Job's friends giving bad advice? That's my social media network telling me to "just pivot," as if pivoting a failing business is as simple as changing lanes. "Have you thought about blockchain?" they ask, like blockchain is magic fairy dust that fixes everything.

Last week, a connection from my Singapore days messaged me: "Have you considered AI integration?"

Brother, I'm trying to make payroll. I'm not trying to integrate anything except my checking and savings accounts to cover bills.

Another guy: "You should do a webinar series!"

About what? "How to Lose Everything in Ten Easy Steps?" "Bankruptcy for Beginners?" "Faith When Your Business Is Failing: A Masterclass in Desperation?"

Paul's thorn in the flesh? That's my guilt from the Caribbean that never fully goes away, the chronic back pain from too many international flights, the anxiety that wakes me at 2 AM wondering if I'm going to lose everything again.

David's cry of "How long, O Lord?" That's me every morning, checking my bank balance, wondering how long I can keep this thing afloat.

R - Reflect Personally: This is where I journal. Messy, honest, sometimes angry words. Questions like: "Where do I see myself in this story?" Last week, I wrote three pages about feeling like Jonah in the belly of a great fish, except my "fish" isn't made of scales and saltwater. It's a failing product launch, and twelve people counting on me for their paychecks.

The journal entry from October 10, 2023, written at 2:37 AM, because sleep is for people without failing businesses:

"God, I feel like Jonah, except I didn't run from You, I ran toward what I thought You wanted. Built this business. Hired these people. Made promises I can't keep. Now I'm in the belly of failure, and it stinks like dead fish and broken dreams. Jonah at least knew why he was there. I have no idea what I did wrong. Followed all the formulas. Prayed all the prayers. Tithed even when it hurt. Still ended up in the whale.

Is this redirection or punishment? Are You trying to get me to

Nineveh or just trying to get my attention? Because You have it. I'm listening. I just don't know what You're saying."

Three pages of that. My handwriting getting worse as the anger increased. By page three, it's just scrawled profanity directed at the situation, not at God, but close enough to make me feel guilty. Then, at the bottom, in different ink from the next morning, "Jonah got vomited onto dry land. Maybe that's what this is, divine vomit leading to divine purpose."

"God, are You trying to redirect me like You did Jonah? Or is this just the consequence of living in a broken world? How do I know the difference?"

I - Implement Practically: "Faith without works is dead (James 2:17, NIV). So, what's the next right thing?

When I studied Joseph forgiving his brothers, I realized forgiveness isn't about restoring relationships. It's about releasing debts you're tired of collecting. So, I wrote three letters. One to my father. One to each ex-wife. One to myself. Burned them all in my garage at 3 AM, watched decades of resentment turn to smoke.

The hardest one to write was to my father, on legal pad paper, because that's what was in my desk:

'Dad,

You're still in that La Porte house. I drove by last week. The lawn's perfect. The roof's new. Everything maintained except what mattered.

I forgive you for doing what you knew—working harder when Mom left because fixing things was the only way you knew to keep life from falling apart. You taught me that real men solve problems, even when the problems are people. You showed love through long shifts and calloused hands, through socket wrenches and quiet sacrifice. I used to think that training only built walls between us, but now I see it built something else too—a kind of endurance I didn't understand until much later. Thank you for that.

For the double shifts that paid for my truck. For showing up to my games with electrical tape still under your fingernails. And for that one time—just once—when you mentioned Job while we were fixing my Isuzu's alternator. Oil on our hands. You weren't even looking at me. But that throwaway comment about believing when nothing makes sense? It's still keeping me afloat.

Your son (more like you than either of us would have thought),

Simon

P.S. Found your antidepressants in the toolbox. Hidden behind the socket set. Still in the pharmacy bag from 2018. I understand now why you never took them. We're both too stubborn to admit we need saving.'

The letter to myself came harder. Ink blurred before I even finished the first sentence.

I forgive you for being human. For that split second of ordinary distraction. For being on that exact stretch of road at that exact moment when the universe collapsed into impact. For surviving when he didn't. For carrying his last breath inside your every breath since.

I forgive you for not being God.

The garage still smells like burned paper. The ashes are still in a coffee can on my workbench. Sometimes I look at them and think, "This is what grace looks like." Not pretty. Not clean. Just the remnants of everything you couldn't carry anymore, finally set free.

P - Persist Through Practice: This is the hardest part. Showing up when you feel nothing. When the Bible feels like cardboard in your mouth, when prayer feels like talking to the ceiling, but I've learned that faithfulness is like working out; you don't feel stronger while you're doing it. You feel stronger weeks later when you realize you're carrying weight that would have crushed you before.

My prayer log from September (yes, I keep a spreadsheet for prayer, don't judge):

- September 1-7: Prayed 3 out of 7 days

- September 8-14: Prayed 2 out of 7 days

- September 15-21: Prayed 1 out of 7 days (and that was just "help")

- September 22-28: Prayed 0 out of 7 days

- September 29: Stefaniya asked if I was okay. I wasn't.

- September 30: Prayed. Just one word: "Please."

- October 1-now: Every single day. Not because I feel spiritual. Because I'll die if I don't.

The Real-World Laboratory

Last month, I was reading about Paul and Silas in prison, singing hymns after being beaten (Acts 16:25). My first thought: "That's insane." My second thought: "That's exactly what insane faith looks like."

I was reading this while sitting in my truck outside our bank. Had just learned we were sixty days from foreclosure. Sixty. Days. The number kept bouncing around my head like a pinball.

Paul and Silas, backs bleeding from Roman whips, shackled in stocks, singing hymns at midnight. Meanwhile, I'm in an air-conditioned truck, no physical wounds, completely free, and I can't even mumble a "thank you" to God.

The contrast was so absurd I actually laughed. The guy walking his dog looked at me like I was losing it. Maybe I was.

That same week, my biggest client—40% of my revenue—pulled out of our contract. Three years of relationship building, gone in a fifteen-minute Zoom call. "We're going in a different direction." Corporate speak for "You're fired."

Halston Dynamics. Mark Halston, the CEO—the man I'd taken to Mavericks games, whose daughter's wedding I'd attended, who called me "brother" every time we talked. The Zoom call was set for thirty minutes. He logged off after twelve.

"Simon, I hate to do this, but..."

Everything after "but" is just noise when someone's firing you.

The contract was worth $380,000 annually. That's $31,666 per month. $7,307 per week. $1,041 per day. I did the math obsessively, like knowing the exact amount of loss would somehow reduce it.

That night, instead of reaching for the Macallan 18 I keep for emergencies (and everything feels like an emergency these days), I reached for my guitar. Started playing "How Great Thou Art" badly, because I haven't practiced in years. Stefaniya came downstairs, probably to tell me to keep it down because the kids were sleeping. Instead, she sat next to me and started singing in Ukrainian.

The guitar, an Ibanez JS1000, I bought in 2004 with my first bonus check. $2,400 I definitely couldn't afford but convinced myself was an "investment." The frets are worn, the finish is cracked, and the G string always goes flat. But that night, with Stefaniya singing words I couldn't understand in a language that sounded like prayer itself, it sounded perfect.

Our kids came downstairs. Alex first, rubbing his eyes. "Why are you singing in the dark?"

We hadn't turned on the lights. Hadn't noticed.

Evan next, dragging his blanket. "Is this church?"

"Kind of," Stefaniya said.

I was playing when Olivia wandered over, climbed into my lap, and fell asleep against my chest. I stopped strumming and just held her there, her breathing soft and steady, the guitar silent between us.

Was it a miracle? No. Halston didn't call back. The contract didn't resurrect. But something shifted. For those few minutes, singing poorly in two languages, we were Paul and Silas in prison, choosing worship over worry.

Scripture as Anchor in the Storm

The book of Hebrews calls hope "an anchor for the soul, firm and secure" (Hebrews 6:19, NIV). I used to think that was a nice metaphor. Now I understand it's survival equipment.

I actually looked up anchor specifications after reading this. A proper anchor for a forty-foot boat weighs about sixty pounds and can hold against 4,000 pounds of force. The anchor doesn't stop the storm or calm the waves. It just keeps you from drifting into the rocks.

That's what Scripture has become, not a solution but a position. Not escape but anchorage.

When my business started failing, really failing, not just struggling but actively dying, I found myself in 2 Corinthians 4: "We are hard pressed on every side, but not crushed; perplexed, but not in despair; persecuted, but not abandoned; struck down, but not destroyed" (vv. 8-9, NIV).

Paul isn't saying we won't be pressed, perplexed, persecuted, or struck down. He's saying those things don't get the final word. There's a "but not" that follows every disaster. Pressed but not crushed—there's still shape to us. Perplexed but not in despair—confusion isn't a conclusion. Struck down but not destroyed—we might be on the ground, but we're still breathing.

I wrote those verses on index cards and put them everywhere:

- Bathroom mirror (scared Stefaniya the first morning)
- Dashboard (cop asked about it during a traffic stop)
- Wallet (falls out every time I pay for something)
- Coffee maker (got wet, ink ran, still readable)
- Computer monitor (IT guy at the coworking space asked if I was okay)
- Inside my shoe (don't ask)

The index cards are from Walmart. $3.97 for 300. I've used 47 so far. At this rate, I'll need more before this is over. That's either faith or insanity. Maybe both.

The Unexpected Gift of Lament

Here's something American Christianity doesn't teach well: how to lament. We're so focused on victory, on breakthrough, on "more than conquerors" that we skip over the fact that over a third of the Psalms are laments. God gave us an entire book, Lamentations, dedicated to grief.

I discovered Lamentations by accident. Was looking for Leviticus (don't judge, I'm still learning where everything is) and landed in Lamentations instead. First verse: "How deserted lies the city, once so full of people!"

I was sitting in my truck in the parking lot of a coworking space that used to be full but was now mostly empty because half the startups had failed. The synchronicity was too perfect, God using my own confusion with Scripture to land me exactly where I needed to be.

Jeremiah writes, "I remember my affliction and my wandering, the bitterness and the gall. I well remember them, and my soul is downcast within me" (Lamentations 3:19-20, NIV). That's in the Bible. The prophet admitting his soul is downcast. Not "was" downcast but "is" downcast. Present tense depression.

I highlighted this so hard I tore through three pages. Stefaniya found me at my desk, yellow highlighter in hand, tears running down my face.

"What's wrong?" she asked.

"Jeremiah is depressed," I said. "The prophet. God's spokesman. Depressed. It's right here in the Bible."

She looked at me like maybe I was having a breakdown. Maybe I was. But it was a breakthrough breakdown, the realization that feeling downcast doesn't disqualify you from faith. It might actually qualify you for deeper faith.

But then, in the very next verse: "Yet this I call to mind and therefore I have hope: Because of the LORD's great love we are not consumed, for his compassions never fail" (Lamentations 3:21–22, NIV).

"Yet." Such a small word carrying such enormous weight. Not "therefore" as if hope logically follows from affliction. But "yet" despite, nevertheless, against all evidence. Yet I have hope.

When Scripture Becomes Survival

Three months ago, sitting in my office with foreclosure notices and final warnings scattered across my desk like accusations, I opened to Isaiah 43. I don't know why that book, that chapter. Sometimes the Spirit leads, sometimes desperation chooses.

The foreclosure notice was printed on yellow paper. Apparently, that's legally required in Texas; public notices must be on colored paper. Like shame needs highlighting. It was dated October 3, giving us until December 3 to figure something out. Sixty days that felt like sixty seconds and sixty years simultaneously.

The other papers: final notice from American Express ($12,847), final notice from the electric company ($487), past due from our health insurance ($2,100), and a handwritten note from our lawn guy saying he couldn't work for free anymore, but "God bless."

"When you pass through the waters, I will be with you; and when you pass through the rivers, they will not sweep over you. When you walk through the fire, you will not be burned" (Isaiah 43:2, NIV).

Notice God doesn't say "if" you pass through waters. He says "when." He doesn't promise to build a bridge over the river or install air conditioning in the fire. He promises presence. "I will be with you."

I sat there surrounded by yellow shame and red warnings and realized maybe presence is enough. Not enough to fix everything, but enough to survive it.

I actually got in the shower fully clothed that night. Don't know why. Just needed to feel water that wasn't drowning me. Stood there in jeans and a t-shirt, letting hot water run over me, whispering Isaiah 43:2 over and over. Stefaniya found me an hour later, still there, water long gone cold.

"Are you okay?" she asked.

"No," I said. "But God is with me in the not-okay."

She got in with me, fully clothed. We stood there, two idiots in wet clothes in a cold shower, holding each other and laughing at the absurdity of it all. The kids found us there. Instead of asking questions, they got in, too, clothes and all.

Five people in a shower meant for two, water barely reaching anyone, laughing like maniacs. The neighbors probably thought we'd lost it. We had. But we'd found something else, the presence that doesn't fix problems but makes them bearable.

The Anchor Holds

I'm writing this from the same office where this chapter started. The storm has passed, but the problems remain. The business might not survive, probably won't, if I'm honest. The stress is real. The bills are real. The possibility of losing everything we've built is real.

Update since I started writing this chapter:

- Lost two more clients

- Had to lay off three people (cried after each conversation)

- Stefaniya started working night shifts at the hospital

- We're selling the good car

139

- Alex asked why we're eating so much spaghetti (it's cheap)
- I'm forty pounds heavier from stress eating
- My back hurts constantly
- I haven't slept through the night in four months

But something's different. I'm different.

Every morning, I open that worn Bible. Every morning, I wrestle with ancient words that somehow speak to modern problems. Every morning, I choose to believe that the God who sustained Job through catastrophe, Paul through imprisonment, and David through years of running is the same God who sees me in my Texas suburb, trying to hold it all together with duct tape and prayer.

This morning's reading: Psalm 46:10, "Be still, and know that I am God."

My translation: "Stop trying to fix everything, Simon. I'm still God even when your business fails."

Easier read than done. But I'm trying.

The mockingbird outside started singing again. Still wet, still small, but singing, nonetheless. Maybe that's what faith looks like. Not escape from the storm, but a song in the middle of it. Not explanations for why the storm came, but presence in the midst of it.

YOUR NEXT STEP

Choose one verse this week. Just one. Not a whole chapter, not a reading plan that you'll abandon by Thursday. One verse. Write it on three index cards. Put them where you'll see them: the mirror, the dashboard, the wallet. Don't try to memorize it through repetition. Just let it marinate. Let ancient words speak to modern problems.

Here's mine for this week: "The LORD is close to the brokenhearted and saves those who are crushed in spirit" (Psalm 34:18, NIV).

I've written it seventeen times so far. Once on the bathroom mirror with Stefaniya's lipstick (she was not happy). Once in the dust on my truck windshield. Once in an email to myself with the subject line "REMEMBER THIS." Once on my hand with a Sharpie before an important call.

Not because writing it more makes it more true, but because I need constant reminders that crushed doesn't mean abandoned.

Scripture isn't magic. It won't make your problems disappear. But it will anchor you when everything else is shifting sand. It will remind you that others have walked this path and survived. It will whisper, in the middle of your storm, that you're not alone, you're not forgotten, and this isn't the end of your story.

Yesterday, Jim Patterson from next door brought over a bird feeder. Said the mockingbirds needed somewhere safe to eat during storms. We hung it outside my office window. This morning, five birds were there, singing while eating.

"Faith is like that," Jim said. "Singing with your mouth full of seeds you didn't plant, trusting more will come tomorrow."

For a retired middle school English teacher from Ohio, that's pretty profound.

The anchor holds. Even when the ship feels like it's breaking apart. Even when you can see the rocks. Even when other boats are sinking all around you. The anchor holds.

Write your verse. Put it where you'll see it. Let God's ancient words speak to your modern mess.

The storm will pass or it won't. The business will survive or it won't. But you will. Because the anchor holds.

CHAPTER SEVEN

Divine Perspective

How to Turn Setbacks into Setups for Growth

I keep a photo on my desk from Easter 2015, my forehead pressed against the Western Wall, prayer tucked between ancient stones. The picture was taken by a stranger—an elderly Jewish man who saw me standing there, probably looking lost—and gestured for me to hand over my phone. "You'll want to remember this," he said in accented English. He was right, though not for the reasons I thought at the time.

The man's name was Mordechai. Found that out because he accidentally took seventeen photos trying to figure out my iPhone. In one, you can see his thumb. In another, just sky. Photo number fourteen is the keeper, me looking like I'm trying to push through the wall with my forehead, which honestly wasn't far from the truth. I was trying to push through to God, wherever He was hiding.

Mordechai wore a black coat despite the April heat, maybe seventy-five degrees. His beard was yellowed at the bottom from decades of cigarettes. When he handed my phone back, he said something in Hebrew, then translated: "The wall doesn't move. But sometimes we need to press against immovable things to find out we can move."

I think about that a lot. Probably more than he intended when he said it.

That photo reminds me daily that God's plan often emerges from our deepest pain, even pain we've carried for decades. Sometimes we have to travel halfway around the world to find out God's been waiting for us all along. Sometimes we have to lose everything we thought mattered to discover what actually does.

For years after the accident, I wrestled with God like Jacob at Peniel. Except Jacob got a new name and a blessing. I got silence and insomnia. I remember sitting in my Kowloon apartment at 3 AM, always 3 AM, like that's when the veil between heaven and earth is thinnest—or maybe just when our defenses are lowest—arguing with the ceiling.

The ceiling had water stains that looked like a map of somewhere I'd never been. I named them. The big one near the window was "Australia." The smaller one by the light fixture was "Madagascar." I'd lie there, counting the stains, thirteen total, like naming my grief would make it smaller.

My upstairs neighbor worked night shifts at the port. He'd come home at 3:30 AM, shower, make what sounded like a seven-course meal, then watch Chinese game shows until dawn. The sound of his footsteps became my countdown clock. If I could argue with God until I heard those footsteps, maybe I'd finally get an answer.

"You could have stopped it," I'd whisper into the darkness, afraid to say it louder, as if volume would make it more blasphemous. "One second. That's all it would have taken. One second earlier or later, and that man goes home to his family. One second, and I'm not carrying this for the rest of my life."

The silence that answered felt heavier than the humidity pressing through my single-pane windows. Hong Kong summers are brutal, the air so thick you feel like you're breathing soup. But that silence was thicker, pressing down on my chest like the weight of unanswered prayers.

I actually timed it once. How long one second really is. Set my phone timer. One Mississippi. That's it. The space between a man living and dying. The gap between me being just another tourist and becoming someone who'd taken a life. One second. Less time than it takes to sneeze.

The Gift Nobody Wants

On Wednesday, October 9, 2024, to be exact, I was helping Alex with his homework, basic addition that felt like advanced calculus to his young mind, when he asked me point-blank: "Daddy, why did God let that man die in your accident?"

We were at the kitchen table, the one we bought at a garage sale for $75. It wobbles unless you put a folded napkin under the left leg. Alex had Graham Cracker crumbs on his worksheet. Problem number seven: "If Steven has three apples and Sarah gives him four more, how many apples does Steven have?"

Alex wasn't looking at the problem. He was looking at me with those eyes that are exactly like mine, brown with a slight ring of dark green around the pupil. Stefaniya calls them "mood ring eyes" because they change color when we cry.

Kids have this surgical precision with questions. No anesthesia. Just straight to the nerve.

I set down his pencil, Dixon Ticonderoga #2, the good kind that actually erases, those cartoon bears holding numbers looking absurdly cheerful for the conversation we were about to have. How do you explain theodicy to a soon-to-be six-year-old? How do you tell him that Daddy asks the same question every day?

145

"You know when I traveled to Turkey for work?" I said, buying time while my brain scrambled for age-appropriate theology. "I walked the same streets where Paul, the guy who wrote parts of the Bible, used to preach. The stones were so smooth from millions of feet walking on them for thousands of years."

The trip to Ephesus, October 2019. Pre-COVID, when we still shook hands with strangers and shared armrests on planes. I'd touched those stones, worn smooth as glass. Our guide, Mehmet, kept saying "Two thousand years of footsteps" as if it were his catchphrase. Probably was. Probably said it to every tour group. But standing there, feeling those smooth stones through my Nike Air Max—terrible for archaeological sites—I got it.

He scrunched his nose, that expression that means he's either thinking hard or needs to use the bathroom. "So?"

"So those stones started out rough. Sharp edges. Uncomfortable to walk on. But every footstep wore them down a tiny bit. Now they're smooth. That's what pain does to us sometimes. It wears down our sharp edges."

"So, God makes bad things happen to make us smoother?"

"No, buddy. Bad things happen because the world is broken. But God doesn't waste them. He uses them to shape us into who we're meant to be."

He thought about it, pencil tapping against his worksheet. "Like when I broke my Lego spaceship and we built a robot instead?"

The spaceship in question: LEGO set #60354, Mars Research Shuttle. $39.99 at Target. Took us three hours to build. He knocked it off his dresser, reaching for a book. Cried for twenty minutes. Then we sat on his bedroom floor, surrounded by plastic debris, and built something that looked like a robot having an existential crisis. He named it "Breaking Bad Robot" because he'd overheard me watching the show. Still don't know how to explain that one to his teacher.

"Exactly like that."

Sometimes five-year-olds understand theology better than seminary professors.

When Suffering Becomes Your Curriculum Vitae

That conversation took me back to a moment in a Trinidad boardroom in 2009. I was pitching a multimillion-dollar infrastructure contract, wearing my best suit—the one I'd bought in Hong Kong for more than most people's mortgage payments. PowerPoint slides are perfectly designed. Financial projections triple-checked. I was in the zone, that flow state where words come easily and confidence radiates.

The suit: Ermenegildo Zegna, charcoal gray, $3,200 from the Pacific Place mall in Admiralty. I'd justified it as an investment. "Dress for the job you want," and all that garbage we tell ourselves when we're using material things to fill spiritual holes. The tie was Hermès, orange with little blue horses, $195. My shoes were Allen Edmonds Park Avenues, $445, polished until you could use them as mirrors.

The boardroom was on the seventeenth floor of the Hyatt Regency Trinidad. Through the windows, you could see the Brian Lara Promenade and beyond that, the Gulf of Paria. The AC was set to "arctic tundra" because that's how they do business in the Caribbean: prove you can afford to freeze.

Right in the middle of my presentation, the CEO—a woman named Patricia with eyes that seemed to see through everything—

stopped me.

"Mr. Rockwell," she said, leaning back in her chair with this knowing look, "you carry yourself like a man who's been broken and rebuilt. That's exactly who we need for this project."

Patricia Williams-Baptiste. Five-foot-two in heels. Harvard MBA, class of '88. Her white suit stayed immaculate, even in the thick Trinidad humidity. On her wall hung a photo of her with President Obama at an economic forum, framed beside a child's drawing of a stick figure labeled *MOMMY THE BOSS* in green crayon.

She had this way of taking off her glasses—red frames, probably cost more than my tie—and cleaning them while she processed information. Power move disguised as maintenance.

I stood there, laser pointer still in hand, completely thrown. "I'm sorry?"

"This project," she gestured to my beautiful slides, "isn't about perfect plans. It's about adapting when everything goes wrong. It's about leading through crisis. And you," she pointed at me with her Mont Blanc pen, "you have the look of someone who knows how to navigate disaster."

The pen was white with gold trim. I remember because she kept clicking it, three clicks, pause, three clicks, pause, while I stood there trying to figure out if I'd just been complimented or called out.

"Your presentation is flawless," she continued. Too flawless. Like you're covering something. But when you talk about risk mitigation, your whole body changes. You lean forward. Your voice drops. You stop using corporate-speak and start using words like 'when things go sideways' and 'damage control.' That's experience talking, not theory."

I got the contract. Not despite my scars, but because of what they'd taught me about resilience. Not because I had all the answers, but because I knew how to keep moving when there weren't any.

The contract was worth $4.7 million over three years. We celebrated at Veni Mangé, this little restaurant on Ariapita Avenue. Patricia ordered for the table, callaloo, roti, doubles, things I couldn't pronounce but tasted like victory. She raised her Carib beer and said, "To broken people building unbreakable things."

Later, much later, after the project succeeded and we'd become something like friends, she told me she'd almost died in a car accident at twenty-three. Spent six months relearning to walk. "I can spot survivor's guilt at fifty paces," she said. "It walks differently. Careful, like the ground might disappear. But also determined, like you've got something to prove to death itself."

When Your Foundation Cracks

I've been baptized three times. Let that sink in. Three times. Once, as a baby at our little Episcopal church in La Porte, where the Reverend probably wondered why this premature infant looked like a tiny orangutan with all that hair. My mother insisted on doing it early, 51 days old, because I'd been born so premature she was afraid of losing me to sudden infant death syndrome or any of the other terrors that haunt new parents.

The Episcopal Church of St. John the Divine, built in the 1950s, has white clapboard siding that needs repainting every 3 years due to the Gulf Coast humidity. The baptismal font was marble, donated by a local family after their son died in Vietnam. There's a plaque, but the letters have worn down so now it just says "In ving mory of" and then his name, still clear as day: "Michael J. Hutcherson, 1952–1970."

Mom kept my baptism certificate in her jewelry box between her mother's pearl necklace and my dad's class ring. The paper's yellowed now, Reverend Morrison's signature faded to brown. He died when I was twelve. At his funeral, his widow said he'd baptized over 300 babies. I wonder how many of us turned out okay.

Once in the LDS church in 2000, when I thought I'd finally found the answer. Full immersion in that chapel baptismal font, the water exactly 98.6 degrees (they have specifications for everything), wearing all white, feeling like this time it would stick. This time I'd be clean. This time, the guilt would wash away with the chlorinated water.

The Copperfield Ward, Houston Texas North Stake. Bishop Anderson did the baptism. He was six-foot-four, I'm five-eleven. When he lowered me backward into the water, my feet came off the bottom. For a second, I panicked, that primal fear of drowning. Then I thought: maybe drowning is exactly what needs to happen. Death to the old self and all that.

The water smelled like a public pool. Someone's kid had thrown up in the men's changing room, and you could smell the Lysol they'd used to clean it. My white jumpsuit was size XL, but still too tight in the shoulders. When I came up from the water, the first thing I saw was Elizabeth smiling, tears running down her face. She thought we'd finally gotten it right. We divorced seven years later.

And once in an ocean of consequences I never saw coming.

The third baptism happened in that Caribbean police station. No water except the sweat running down my back despite the aggressive air conditioning. No ceremony except the ritual of repeating my statement again and again. No witnesses except an exhausted detective who'd seen too many tourist accidents to be shocked by another one.

Detective Williams had a photo on his desk: him, much younger, in a British police uniform, with a full head of hair. "Scotland Yard, 1979-1987," he said when he caught me looking. "Came here for vacation, never left. Island does that to some people."

The police station was painted that particular shade of institutional green, found nowhere in nature. The floor was linoleum, curling at the corners. Someone had tried to make it cheerier by hanging travel posters, "Discover Paradise!" which felt like a mockery given why I was there.

Williams offered me coffee from a Mr. Coffee machine that looked older than me. It came in a mug that said, "Keep Calm and Carry On," though most of the letters had faded, so it just read "eep alm and Car y On."

Just me, those fluorescent lights that made everything look guilty, and a detective asking me to describe again how the accident happened. Each retelling felt like drowning. Each "I didn't see him in time" pulled me deeper under waves of guilt. Each "dark clothing, outside the crosswalk" felt like I was trying to excuse the inexcusable.

That's when I learned that some baptisms take place in tears rather than water. Some conversions take place in courtrooms rather than in churches. Some people meet God not in glory but in guilt.

The View from Rock Bottom

Want to know something about hitting bottom? It's surprisingly solid. I discovered this at 2:47 AM on May 5, 2012, sitting on the floor of a 7-Eleven bathroom in Lan Kwai Fong, Hong Kong's party district. The floor was that particular kind of dirty that comes from thousands of drunk people making bad decisions. I fit right in.

The 7-Eleven sat on D'Aguilar Street, wedged between a bar called Tequila Jack's and a kebab shop that didn't close until sunrise. The bathroom was so small that you could touch both walls without stretching your arms. On the door, someone had scrawled "CALL JENNY FOR A GOOD TIME." Beneath it, another hand had replied, "Jenny is my mom, you sick fool."

I stared at it for a moment, wondering, not just why it was written in English, but what kind of ache makes people reach for a wall to say something no one asked to hear.

The toilet paper dispenser was broken and held closed with duct tape. The mirror had a crack running diagonally from corner to corner, splitting my reflection into two uneven pieces. Fitting.

My second divorce had just been finalized. The papers were in my jacket pocket, folded so many times they were starting to tear at the creases. I'd just lost another business deal, this one to a younger, hungrier competitor who reminded me of myself twenty years ago, before life had beaten the shine off. I couldn't stop shaking. Not from the cold—Hong Kong in May is warm enough. From the complete collapse of everything I'd built my identity on.

The competitor's name was Marcus Chen, twenty-eight, Stanford MBA, the kind of guy who ran marathons "for fun" and had an Instagram full of sunrise photos from mountain peaks. His presentation came right after mine. Where I'd shown experience and careful planning, he'd shown hunger and innovation. The client, a logistics firm looking to expand into Southeast Asia, chose hunger.

"We appreciate your experience, Simon," they'd said, that tone that means you're about to get the corporate kiss-off, "but we're looking for fresh perspectives."

Fresh. Like I was expired milk.

A store clerk knocked on the door, rapid Cantonese that I couldn't understand, but recognized the tone: "Are you okay in there?" The universal sound of minimum-wage concern.

I bought a Pocari Sweat and a Snickers bar on my way out, $31 HKD. The clerk, a young kid with anime hair, didn't make eye contact. He'd seen too many broken expats stumble through at 3 AM to care about another one.

Outside, Lan Kwai Fong was still raging. Twenty-somethings in too-short dresses and too-tight shirts, spending money they didn't have on drinks they wouldn't remember. I stood there, forty-three years old, holding my convenience store dinner, watching kids live the life I'd thought would save me at their age.

That's when I realized: I'd spent years running. La Porte to Philadelphia for college. Philadelphia to San Diego for the first real job. San Diego to Singapore for the bigger opportunity. Singapore to Hong Kong for a fresh start. But you can't outrun what lives inside your ribcage. You can't use geography to escape guilt that's encoded in your DNA.

Your Trials Are Not Your Identity

I used to practice my introduction in hotel mirrors before networking events. "Hi, I'm Simon, an international business consultant specializing in infrastructure development." Never "Hi, I'm Simon, the guy who killed someone in an accident." Never "Hi, I'm Simon, twice divorced and spiritually homeless." But that's who I saw in the reflection, not the successful businessman but the broken man underneath the expensive suit.

The Marriott in Shenzhen had the worst mirrors—fluorescent lighting that showed every pore, every regret. I'd stand there at 6 AM, trying different smiles. Professional smile. Confident smile. "I'm totally fine," smile. They all looked like hostages trying to signal for help.

One morning, hangover making my reflection look like a police sketch, I tried the truth: "Hi, I'm Simon, and I'm a mess pretending to be a businessman." The reflection didn't argue.

Joseph's brothers meant evil when they sold him into slavery, but God meant it for good (Genesis 50:20, NIV). I used to hate that verse. It felt like divine gaslighting when well-meaning church folks quoted it at me. "Everything happens for a reason," they'd say, patting my shoulder with that particular Christian combination of compassion and condescension. I wanted to scream, "What possible reason justifies a family losing someone they love?"

The worst was Linda from the Houston church. Sweet woman made cookies for every funeral but had the theological sensitivity of a sledgehammer. "God needed him in heaven," she said once, apropos of nothing, while we were setting up chairs for Bible study.

"God needs a maintenance supervisor?" I asked. "Heaven's got plumbing issues?"

She looked at me like I'd blasphemed, which I probably had. But seriously, God, omnipotent creator of the universe, needs a forty-three-year-old father of two to fix something in paradise? The logic breaks down faster than my second marriage.

Now I understand differently. God didn't cause my rental car to hit that man. God didn't plan for someone to lose their life that night. But He refused to let it be wasted. Every scar became a story. Every wound, eventually, became a well from which others could drink.

Practical Steps for the Practically Broken

Living in Hong Kong was where I first learned about the art of repairing broken pottery with gold, a tradition more often associated with Japan but one that is also embraced across cultures. Americans want everything fixed yesterday, invisible, like it never happened. We reach for clear glue and hope nobody notices the cracks. But the Cantonese seemed to understand this truth instinctively: some things are more beautiful for having been broken. The gold doesn't hide the fracture; it highlights it. It says, "Something happened here, and we chose to make it beautiful."

I bought a bowl from a night market in Mong Kok. Blue ceramic with white cranes painted on it. HK$200, probably worth HK$20. The first week I had it, I knocked it off my kitchen counter while reaching for instant noodles at 2 AM. It broke into five pieces.

Found a repair shop in Sheung Wan, an old man who looked like he'd been fixing things since the British handed Hong Kong back. He looked at my broken bowl and said in English, "You want invisible fix?"

"No," I said, surprising myself. "Make it obvious."

He smiled. Took two weeks. It costs HK$500 to fix a HK$200 bowl. Now it sits on my desk in Texas, gold veins running through it like a map of recovery. Alex asked why I keep a broken bowl on my desk. I told him, "To remember that broken things can become art."

My life is held together with theological gold paste, and I'm learning to stop hiding the seams.

Here's what actually works when life feels like a dumpster fire in a hurricane:

Daily Non-Negotiables

Coffee with God before coffee with anyone else. I use the same mug every morning, chipped handle, faded "World's Best Dad" that my kids gave me, coffee stains that won't come out no matter how much I scrub. I talk to Him like He's sitting across the table because, theologically speaking, He is. Some mornings, it's deep theology about providence and free will. Some mornings it's just "Help." Both count.

Yesterday's conversation: "God, the Astros lost again. I know there's war and famine and real problems, but I'm starting to think You're a Rangers fan, and that feels personal."

Silence.

"Also, my back hurts, Alex needs braces we can't afford, and I think the cat has diabetes. The cat. Diabetes. Is this cosmic comedy?"

More silence, but warmer somehow. Like God's chuckling at my priorities.

Write down three things that didn't suck today. I keep a notebook by my bed, not my phone, that's a portal to anxiety. Yesterday mine were: "Stefaniya made borscht" (her grandmother's recipe, tastes like love and beets), "Nobody got pink eye" (it was going around my son's school like wildfire), and "Found my reading glasses in the refrigerator" (still don't know how they got there, but at least I found them).

The notebook is a Moleskine knockoff from Target, $3.99. The pen is a Bic that's running out of ink, so some words are more faith than writing. Last week's highlight: "Olivia didn't say the F-word at preschool today." Low bar, but we cleared it.

Move your body. Depression wants you still as a corpse. It whispers lies like "What's the point?" and "Stay in bed where it's safe." Hope moves, even if it's just to the mailbox. Even if it's just standing in the shower. Even if it's just walking to the kitchen to make another pot of coffee. Movement is rebellion against despair.

Your 30-Day Resilience Plan

I developed this after my third (and final, thank God) restart. It's not magic. It's not revolutionary. It's just consistent small actions that compound over time, like interest, but for your soul.

I wrote this plan on the back of a Chili's menu while waiting for my to-go order. Chicken crispers, ranch dressing, pretending everything was fine. The waitress saw me scribbling and asked if I was a writer. "No," I said, "I'm just trying to figure out how not to fall apart." She brought me free chips and salsa. Sometimes strangers are angels in aprons.

Week 1: Acknowledge Reality

• Day 1-3: Write your uncensored story. Not the version you tell at parties. Not the testimony you've sanitized for church. The real one with all the ugly parts.

I wrote mine on my laptop, then my computer crashed before I could save it. Had to write it again by hand. Took seventeen pages of a legal pad. My hand cramped. I cried. I wrote things I'd never said out loud: "I'm glad it wasn't me who died," and "Sometimes I hate God for letting me survive," and "I'm afraid my kids will inherit my broken."

• Day 4-5: Circle the parts that still hurt to read. These are your growth edges.

• Day 6-7: Identify one person to share one circled part with. Just one. Start small.

Week 2: Anchor in Truth

- Choose 3 scriptures that speak to your specific pain

- Write them on index cards (analog matters here, the physical act of writing engages different parts of your brain)

- Put them where you'll see them (mirror, dashboard, wallet)

- Read aloud morning and night, yes, out loud, even if you feel ridiculous

My three:

1. "The LORD is close to the brokenhearted" (Psalm 34:18, NIV) - Bathroom mirror

2. "My grace is sufficient for you" (2 Corinthians 12:9, NIV) - Truck dashboard

3. "I can do all things through Christ" (Philippians 4:13, NIV) - Above the coffee maker

Alex found the one on the bathroom mirror and tried to write his own version underneath it in crayon: "God luvs Dady even wen he yels at cars."

The spelling was a mess, but the message hit harder than any sermon.

Week 3: Take One Small Action

- Identify one person going through similar pain

- Send an encouraging text/email, doesn't have to be profound, just "Thinking of you"

- Offer to meet for coffee, no agenda, just presence

- Share one thing that's helped you. not advice, just "This helped me"

I texted Marcus from the Singapore AA group: "Still sober?" He replied: "47 days." I replied: "Hero." He replied: "Barely holding on." I replied: "That still counts." That's it. Took thirty seconds. He told me later that it kept him from drinking that night.

Week 4: Build Your Protocol

- Morning: 5-minute gratitude practice (even if it's just "Coffee exists")

- Midday: 2-minute breathing prayer (in your car, bathroom, wherever)

- Evening: Journal one way you saw God today (might be tiny, that's okay)

- Weekly: Meet with one person who strengthens your faith

From Surviving to Something More

Three kids call me Daddy now. Every night at bedtime, when my middle one asks me to check for monsters under his bed and in his closet, I tell him the truth: "The only monsters here are the ones Daddy already defeated, and they can't hurt you."

Evan's monster protocol is extensive:

1. Check under bed (use phone flashlight).

2. Check in closet (move all shoes).

3. Check behind door.

4. Check under dirty laundry pile.

5. Spray "monster spray" (water in a spray bottle with a label I made).

6. Say the prayer: "God, please keep the monsters, bad dreams, and spiders away. Especially spiders."

Last night, he added, "Also, check if monsters are hiding in Daddy's feelings."

Kid's too bright for a four-year-old.

He doesn't know I'm talking about the monster of guilt that lived under my bed for twenty years. The monster of shame that hid in my closet. The monster of "not enough" that followed me from continent to continent.

Stefaniya still laughs when I try to pronounce Ukrainian words correctly. "Борщ" (Borscht) comes out sounding like I'm choking. "Спасибі" (thank you) sounds like I'm sneezing. But she laughs with love, not mockery. She chose me not in spite of my broken pieces but because of how they've shaped me. She saw the gold holding me together and decided it was beautiful.

Last week, while teaching Alex Ukrainian numbers, I said "п'ять" (five) and apparently pronounced it like a completely different word that means something inappropriate. Stefaniya laughed so hard she cried. Alex now randomly yells my mispronunciation in public. Parenting is humiliation with snack breaks.

The Mystery of Redemptive Suffering

When I stood at the Church of the Holy Sepulchre on Easter 2015 and touched the stone where tradition says Jesus's body was laid, something shifted in my understanding. This is the God who knows what it's like to have your plans murdered. He knows what it's like to carry scars, even after resurrection, He showed Thomas the wounds. The resurrection didn't erase the nail marks; it transformed them into proof of love.

The stone was cold. Colder than I expected for Jerusalem in April. Polished smooth by millions of hands over centuries. The woman next to me was crying, kissing the stone, speaking Russian or maybe Ukrainian. The man behind me was taking selfies. The priest managing the line looked bored, checking his phone between pilgrims.

I touched it and felt... nothing. No lightning bolt. No divine download. Just cold stone under my palm.

But walking away, I realized that's exactly right. God doesn't live in the spectacular. He lives in cold stone, bored priests, and tourists taking selfies. He lives in the ordinary aftermath of extraordinary suffering.

Your trials aren't cosmic punishment. They're not God's way of teaching you a lesson, like some divine detention. When terrible things happen—accidents, divorces, failures—it's not because God is punishing you. It's because we live in a broken world where broken things happen to broken people.

But here's the mystery: God enters into our brokenness. He doesn't fix it from a distance. He enters it. Inhabits it. Transforms it from the inside.

Three months after the accident, I got a letter. It came through the rental car company's lawyer, from the man's family. It was written in French, and I had to get it translated at a UPS store for forty-five dollars.

"I don't forgive you," they wrote. "Maybe someday. But we want you to know he was walking home from his second job. He was tired. He worked two jobs to pay for our daily living. He was a good man. Remember that."

I carry that letter in my wallet. Next to my kids' photos. A reminder that redemption doesn't erase reality. He was a good man, so it seemed. His family still doesn't have him around. And somehow, God is working even in that.

The path from setback to setup isn't straight. Mine went through forty-nine countries (yes, I counted), three marriages, and one vehicular negligent homicide investigation that still makes my hands shake when I drive at dusk. But every detour taught me something I couldn't learn on the interstate. Every breakdown became building material for a breakthrough.

YOUR NEXT STEP

This week, identify one "setback" from your past. Write down three ways it prepared you for something you couldn't have handled before. Maybe your divorce taught you to spot red flags. Maybe your business failure taught you humility. Maybe your addiction taught you compassion for other strugglers.

Mine from this week: Setback: Lost the Halston contract, which prepared me for:

1. Having honest conversations with my kids about money

2. Appreciating Stefaniya working night shifts without complaint

3. Remembering that my worth isn't my net worth

Then share this with someone who's in their setback right now. Not as advice, nobody wants advice when they're drowning. Share it as testimony: "I survived this. You will too. And you'll be different on the other side, not unscarred, but stronger at the broken places."

Texted Tom from the Dallas men's group yesterday: "Remember

when your wife died and you wanted to die too? Now you're remarried with a new grandbaby. God's not done with your story."

He texted back: "Crying in Home Depot. Thanks for that."

Then: "But yeah. You're right."

Then: "Your story's not done either, brother."

Remember: your worst moment might be preparation for someone else's breakthrough. Your deepest pain might become someone else's lifeline. That's not consolation prize theology. That's the economy of the Kingdom, where nothing is wasted, everything is redeemable, and the last become first.

Even you. Especially you.

I'm writing this at 4:47 AM (yes, that alarm time again). Alex just came downstairs, dragging his Minecraft blanket. "Daddy, why are you crying at your computer?"

"Because sometimes grown-ups have big feelings too."

"Is it about the man from your accident?"

"Yeah, buddy. It is."

He climbed into my lap, fifty pounds of boy and blanket and morning breath. "Maybe he's in heaven teaching God about cars."

"Maybe he is."

"Can we have pancakes?"

From suffering to theology to pancakes in thirty seconds. That's parenting. That's faith. That's life after death, not the afterlife kind, but the kind where you keep living after part of you has died.

The gold holds the cracks together. The cracks tell the story. The story helps others survive their breaking.

That's divine perspective: God doesn't waste anything, not even our waste.

CHAPTER EIGHT

One Church, Many Stories

Global Faith Lessons from Around the World

The text came at 3:47 AM Hong Kong time. Chen's grandmother was dying. The woman who'd taught underground churches in Shanghai by hiding Bible verses in lullabies was dying. I sat on my apartment floor in Kowloon, holding my phone, wondering if I should wake Stefaniya. That's when it hit me: this woman I'd met once had taught me more about resilient faith than twenty years of Sunday school.

The text was in Mandarin. I had to use Google Translate, holding my phone up to the bathroom light because I didn't want to wake Stefaniya. She was seven months pregnant with Alex, snoring that pregnancy snore that sounds like a freight train with allergies.

Chen had written: "奶奶快不行了" which Google said meant "Grandma is dying," but the literal translation was "Grandma can't go on." That felt more accurate. Sometimes we don't die. We just can't go on, and then we stop.

My apartment floor was that fake hardwood laminate, cold even through my socks. The ones with holes in both big toes because I'm too cheap or too lazy to buy new ones. Outside, Hong Kong was doing its 4 AM thing: garbage trucks beeping, early-morning joggers, the constant hum of air conditioners fighting humidity that never quits.

165

Look, I'm gonna be frank with you. I used to think breakthrough meant fixing everything that was broken. Turns out, God's more interested in using the broken pieces.

Let me tell you how I learned this the hard way, across five continents and through more mistakes than any man should make.

When Success Becomes Emptiness: Singapore, 2007

The deal was worth $3.7 million. I remember the exact number because I'd written it on a napkin at the Raffles Hotel bar, circling it three times like it was some holy grail. My hands were shaking, not from nerves, but from exhaustion. I'd been up for thirty-six hours straight, living on black coffee and the adrenaline of closing the biggest deal of my career.

The napkin was from the Long Bar, where they supposedly invented the Singapore Sling. Never had one, too sweet. I was drinking Johnnie Walker Black, neat, at $28 SGD per glass—which is criminal—but everything at Raffles is criminal. The napkin had a little palm tree logo and their tagline: "In the tradition of grand hotels."

I'd ordered room service, $180 SGD for a club sandwich and fries. The fries were cold by the time they arrived, but I was too wired to care. Just sat there, looking at my laptop screen showing the wire confirmation, eating cold fries, feeling like I'd won something I couldn't name.

That's when James knocked on my hotel room door at 2:47 AM with a bottle of Tiger beer and news about his daughter.

James Whitmore, British expat, been in Singapore since 1987. Worked for Barclays, then went independent. Had this habit of loosening his tie exactly three inches when he drank, never took it off, just loosened it precisely three inches. Measured it once with a ruler when he was drunk. Exactly three inches.

He was wearing his funeral suit. I knew because he'd told me about it once: Savile Row, which cost him £3,000 in 1995, and he only wore it to funerals and closings. That night, it was for both.

"Sophie died last year," he said, setting the beer on my desk next to my victory champagne. "Leukemia. I made my first million the same month we buried her."

The air conditioning hummed. Outside, Singapore sparkled like scattered diamonds. Inside, something cracked in me.

"You know what really messed me up?" James continued, his British accent thick with grief. "I thought if I could just hit certain numbers, control certain outcomes, I'd feel... I don't know. Safe? Worthy? But God's accounting system doesn't match ours."

Sophie had been nine. James showed me her photo, school uniform, missing front tooth, and holding a certificate for "Best Speller in Primary 3." He carried it in his wallet, where most people keep credit cards. The edges were soft from handling.

"She wanted to be a marine biologist," he said. "Used to make me watch The Blue Planet on repeat. David Attenborough's voice still makes me cry."

I pushed my laptop aside. The contract I'd been reviewing suddenly looked like hieroglyphics.

"My dad always quoted Ecclesiastes to me," I said. "'Whoever loves money never has enough.' Used to drive me crazy. He was an electrician in La Porte, Texas. What did he know about real money?"

James laughed, but it sounded like breaking glass. "Everything, apparently."

That conversation saved me from twenty years of chasing the wrong definition of success. In twenty minutes, a grieving British father taught me what two decades of American prosperity gospel couldn't: sometimes God saves us from our prayers, not through them.

We finished the Tiger beer, warm and skunky by then, and watched the sun rise over Marina Bay. James fell asleep in the chair, still in his funeral suit, tie loosened exactly three inches. I covered him with the overpriced Raffles bathrobe and let him sleep. When he woke up, he said, "Sophie would have liked you. You're properly broken."

Highest compliment I ever received.

When Pressure Creates Diamonds: Shanghai, 2012

Fast forward five years. Second divorce papers signed. I was back in Asia because apparently, I process pain through airline miles. My colleague Zhang invited me to what he called "a gathering."

Zhang Wei, not his real name, can't use real names when you're talking about underground churches in China. Worked with me at a small engineering firm, shared a cubicle that smelled like instant noodles and desperation. He wore the same three shirts in rotation: blue on Monday, white on Wednesday, and gray on Friday. Tuesday and Thursday were wild cards.

The invitation came during lunch at Mr. Pizza, yes, that's a real chain in China. A Korean-owned pizza place that puts corn and mayonnaise on pizza like that's normal. Zhang leaned over his sweet potato pizza (I'm not making this up) and whispered, "You want to see real faith?"

Can I tell you something I've never written before? I almost didn't go. The apartment building looked abandoned. Graffiti covered the entrance. My palms were sweating as we climbed five flights of stairs in complete darkness.

The building was in Hongkou district, old Shanghai, the kind of place that survived the Cultural Revolution by being too unimportant to demolish. Concrete cancer eating the walls. Electrical wires hanging like party streamers nobody took down. The stairwell smelled like cabbage and cat pee.

Fifth floor, apartment 5-3. The door had seven locks. Seven. Zhang knocked in a pattern, two quick, three slow, one quick. Like Morse code for "let the paranoid foreigner in."

Then I heard it. Children singing.

Twenty-three people crammed into a living room the size of my hotel bathroom. The children were singing Bible verses set to folk melodies. That's when I met Chen's grandmother.

Her name was Chen Mei-Ling, but everyone called her Nǎi Nai, Grandma. Four-foot-eight on a good day, wearing a green sweater with holes in both elbows, house slippers that had seen better decades. Her apartment had one window, facing another building so close you could shake hands with the neighbors. The wallpaper was peeling, showing three different patterns from three different decades, like geological layers of poverty.

She was 87 pounds of pure spiritual dynamite. Her hands looked like tree roots, all knots and veins, but when she traced Bible verses on her palm, her fingers moved like a concert pianist's.

"During the Cultural Revolution," Chen translated as his

169

grandmother spoke, "owning a Bible meant twenty years of hard labor. So, I became a Bible."

She showed us her system. Each finger joint was a verse. Palm lines were chapter divisions. She'd tap them in sequence while cooking, while walking, while pretending to count money at the market. Forty years of muscle memory.

"They burned all the books," she said through Chen. "But they couldn't burn what was in here." She tapped her temple, then her heart.

She'd memorized entire books. Taught them through children's songs, hide-and-seek games, and even recipes. "Add three cups of flour, like the three days in the tomb. Mix thoroughly, like God mixes suffering and glory."

"Your American Christianity," she said through Chen, fixing me with eyes that had seen more than I could imagine, "is like medicine for sadness. But faith here?" She tapped her chest. "Faith here is like... how you say... immunity? Not cure. Survival."

She made us tea, jasmine, loose leaves in glass jars that had once held something else. The cups didn't match. Mine had a chip that would cut my lip if I wasn't careful. The tea was too hot, too strong, perfect.

"You know what they made me write during my re-education?" she asked, pulling out a notebook so old the binding was more tape than thread. Page after page of the same phrase: "Religion is the opium of the people."

"Ten thousand times I wrote this. And every time, I prayed, 'You are not opium. You are oxygen.'"

She spent three years in prison, came out still singing. Me? I'd spent three years in self-imposed spiritual exile after my accident and came out barely breathing.

What I learned in that Shanghai apartment ended up saving me from spiritual suffocation three years later, when my mother's type 1 diabetes took a sharp turn for the worse the week before Stefaniya's wedding. I didn't know it then, but some seasons prepare you for others. Sometimes pressure doesn't crush you. Sometimes it creates diamonds. Chen's grandmother used to say that with a straight face, like she'd lived it. And Paul said it long before either of us were born: "We are hard pressed on every side but not crushed" (2 Corinthians 4:8, NIV).

When Forgiveness Costs Everything: Jerusalem, 2005

You know what's pathetic? Flying to Jerusalem hoping geography could fix what theology couldn't. But there I was, Easter 2005, walking the Via Dolorosa like a spiritual tourist, sweating through my Tommy Bahama shirt.

The shirt was salmon-colored with tiny palm trees. $89 from Macy's, on sale. Completely wrong for Jerusalem in April, too bright, too American, too "I'm having a mid-life crisis and think travel will fix it." I stuck out like a neon sign saying "ROB ME" in three languages.

The Via Dolorosa was packed. Korean church group in matching t-shirts. Russian Orthodox pilgrims carrying a cross that looked heavier than my guilt. Street vendors selling "authentic" crown of thorns made in China. The whole thing felt like Disneyland for the desperate.

Yusuf's shop wasn't in any guidebook. I stumbled in escaping the afternoon heat. The coffee cups were smaller than shot glasses but heavier than they looked, thick ceramic that held heat like grief holds memory.

The shop was more like a cave carved into the Old City walls. No sign, just a green door that didn't quite close. Inside: three tables, six chairs, one cat that looked older than Jerusalem itself. The walls were covered in photos, all football teams, all celebrating something.

Yusuf was maybe sixty, maybe ninety, that ageless quality men get when they've survived everything. White stubble, hands that had done real work, eyes that had cried real tears.

"You look like someone who killed somebody," he said in English that sounded like gravel.

My hands actually shook. How could he know?

"Not with gun," he clarified, studying my face. "With accident. With mistake that follows you."

He was grinding cardamom pods with a mortar and pestle older than America. The smell filled the cave-shop, mixed with tobacco and something else—frankincense, maybe, or just the smell of old stones holding old prayers.

I told him about 1994. The pedestrian. The sound. The guilt that had destroyed two marriages and countless nights of sleep.

Yusuf pulled out a photo. His son wore a Barcelona soccer jersey, number 10. "Amir. Sixteen. Football player, oh, football, you Americans say soccer. Best midfielder in East Jerusalem."

"Second intifada. Wrong corner, wrong moment. The soldier was also sixteen."

The photo was behind cracked glass, the kind of crack that spreads like veins. Amir was mid-kick, ball frozen in space, smile frozen in time. 2000 written in pen on the corner. The year everything changed.

"The soldier, David, his name, he came here. Three years after. Sat where you sit. Cried where you cry."

He poured more coffee. The cardamom made my eyes water. Or maybe it wasn't the cardamom.

"For one year, I made lists. Names. Addresses. Plans. You know what revenge gave me? Diabetes. My wife couldn't look at me. My daughter stopped singing."

"What changed?"

"I read Matthew 18. Peter asks Jesus about forgiveness. Seven times enough? Jesus says seventy-seven. I realized I was drinking poison, waiting for others to die."

He showed me his morning ritual. Two cups, one blue with Arabic script, one white with Hebrew letters. Both chipped, both used daily.

"Every morning, I wake with hate. Normal. I pour coffee in both cups. I drink from both. Jewish coffee, Arab coffee, same coffee. This is my protest. This is my prayer."

He showed me his morning ritual. Two cups. "Every day I choose. Pour poison or pour coffee. This is my worship."

That's when I noticed it. Behind the register, next to Amir's photo: a small Israeli flag and a Palestinian flag, crossed like friends' arms.

Also on that shelf: a photo of David, the soldier. In civilian clothes, holding a baby. "His son," Yusuf said. "Named Amir. He asks permission. I said yes. Maybe this Amir grows up without war in his name."

Three years later, when road rage nearly made me do something stupid on I-35, I remembered Yusuf's cups—pulled over. Chose coffee.

That fifteen-minute lesson in a Jerusalem shop saved me from a lifetime of prison, internal or otherwise.

When Church Transcends Walls: Rio de Janeiro, 2014

The Copacabana Palace Hotel's Wi-Fi crashed during a multimillion-dollar video conference. In 2014, that was like losing oxygen. I stormed out to find an internet café, cursing in three languages.

The languages: English (obviously), Spanish (badly), and Mandarin (just the curse words Zhang taught me). The conference was with South American Petroleum about a pipeline project worth $12.3 million. I was wearing my lucky cufflinks, little oil derricks my first boss gave me in 1997. The Wi-Fi died right as I was screen-sharing the financial projections. Murphy's Law in Portuguese.

The hotel concierge, a kid named Paulo with braces and ambition, pointed me toward an internet café three blocks away. "Very fast, senhor. Gaming café. Kids play Warcraft." Perfect. Nothing says professional like closing deals next to teenagers screaming about dragons.

Maria's laugh stopped me cold.

She was running an online Bible study from a corner table, her laptop screen showing faces from around the world. "Miren, amigos," she was saying, "look at Psalm 137. How do we sing the Lord's song in a strange land?"

Maria Fernandes found out later. Forty-three years old, former Assemblies of God missionary to Angola, back in Brazil because lupus was winning. She had that swollen moon-face from prednisone, joints wrapped in those beige bandages that scream "chronic pain." But her laugh—her laugh—could wake the dead and make them dance samba.

Her laptop was held together with duct tape and prayer. A Toshiba from 2009, keys worn smooth, screen flickering like a disco strobe. She had a USB fan pointed at it to keep it from overheating, and a stack of paper towels for when her water bottle sweated onto the keyboard.

There were forty-three souls gathered online that night. A grandmother in Caracas, five others leaning over her shoulder. Chen from rural China, awake at three in the morning. A family in a Colombian refugee camp, their children curled up on the floor behind them.

The screen was divided into tiny squares, like looking at humanity through a broken kaleidoscope. In one square: an old woman holding her phone with both hands, squinting at the screen. Another: a teenager translating for his parents. Bottom right: someone's ceiling fan because they didn't know their camera was on.

The Colombian family was in a tent. You could see the UNHCR logo on the canvas behind them. The kids were maybe five and seven, wearing donated clothes that didn't fit. The father had his arm in a sling made from a torn t-shirt. They were sharing earbuds, each person getting one ear of God's word.

Maria had been a traditional missionary until lupus grounded her. "I thought God benched me," she told me during break, her breathing labored but eyes bright. "Then I realized, Paul planted churches through letters. I just have better Wi-Fi."

"Better" was relative. The connection dropped every few minutes. She'd freeze mid-sentence, face contorted in some weird expression, then pop back saying "Amen? Amen!" like nothing happened. Everyone would laugh and type "AMEN" in the chat, hearts and praying hands emojis filling the screen.

She showed me her setup: an external keyboard because her hands couldn't handle the laptop keys anymore, a mouse with enlarged buttons, and a Bible app set to 200% font size. "My body is falling apart," she said, "but my ministry is going global. God's humor, no?"

Here's what wrecked me: Sebastian in Venezuela hadn't eaten in two days but wouldn't miss Bible study. Chen risked arrest every login. And Maria? She was dying, literally dying, but teaching about an abundant life.

"You think real church needs walls?" Maria asked. "Tell that to the early Christians in catacombs. Tell that to my friend in Iran who baptizes people in bathtubs. Church isn't a place. It's wherever two or three gather, even if they gather in pixels."

She introduced me to her digital congregation. Each name came with a story. Each story came with scars.

"This is Esperanza 'Hope' in English. Her husband disappeared three months ago. Secret police, we think. Still prays for his return at every meeting. This is Ahmed. Muslim background believer. His family held his funeral, literally buried an empty coffin. In their eyes, he's dead. In Christ's eyes, he's finally alive."

She pointed to a black square, no video. "That's Lin. No one knows where Lin is logging in from. Never shows a face, never uses a real name. Types prayers in code. Could be anyone, anywhere. But every week, like clockwork: 'Still here. Still believing.'"

"This is Esperanza. Her husband disappeared three months ago. Still prays for his return at every meeting. This is Ahmed. Muslim background believer. His family thinks he's dead. In a way, he is. Dead to old life, alive in Christ."

When I complained about slow internet destroying my deal, Maria laughed again. "Your business uses technology for profit. We use it for prophets. Which one lasts longer?"

I missed my conference call. Completely forgot about it, sitting there watching Maria teach about singing in exile to actual exiles. South American Petroleum sent three emails, each more passive-aggressive than the last. Lost the deal. Gained perspective.

Maria died in 2019. COVID, before the vaccines. But her digital church? Still meets. Every Tuesday, 8 PM Brazil time. Sister Esperanza leads now. Her husband never came back, but she did. From student to teacher, from desperate to determined.

That digital church saved my faith two years later during COVID, when every building closed but the Church kept gathering. Maria taught me something that day: ministry isn't about proximity. It's about availability. And sometimes the most powerful miracles happen through the weakest Wi-Fi.

When Strangers Become Family: Hong Kong, 2012-2015

This next part is hard to admit. After my second divorce, I ended up in a Russian church in Hong Kong, where I understood exactly nothing. My Russian vocabulary? "Spasibo," "izvinite," and "ya ne ponimayu," which means "I don't understand."

That last phrase summed up my whole life.

The church met in a community center in Tsim Sha Tsui, sandwiched between a tutoring center and a shop selling questionable electronics. Sunday services at 2 PM because that's when the space was cheapest. Fifty-seven people crammed into a room meant for thirty, singing hymns that sounded like beautiful threats.

The first time I went, I sat in the back, trying to be invisible. Hard to do when you're the only non-Slavic face in the room. A babushka in a purple dress that had seen better decades grabbed my arm, dragged me to the third row. "Sit, sit," she commanded in English that sounded like it hurt to speak.

Why did I keep going back? Because Natalya whispered translations, even though it gave her headaches. Because Viktor's mother mailed black bread from Moscow that he shared like communion. Because Olga prayed over me in Russian, and somehow my spirit understood every word.

Natalya Volkov, thirty-four, taught piano to rich kids in Central during the week, translated God's word to lost Americans on Sundays. She'd lean over during sermons, whispering translations that smelled like lavender and sounded like redemption. "He's saying we're all prodigals... now he's talking about pigs... oh, that's a joke about Putin, ignore that part."

Viktor worked construction, hands like hammers, heart like butter. His mother's black bread came wrapped in Russian newspapers, three-week-old news surrounding week-old bread that somehow tasted fresh. He'd tear off chunks during fellowship, handing them out like he was distributing grace itself.

"God speaks all languages," Viktor would say, his rough hands resting gently on my shoulders. "We pray. He translates."

These people knew exile. Real exile. Not my self-imposed American evangelical wilderness, but the kind where you can't go home because home might kill you. They understood Jeremiah 29:7 in their bones:

"Seek the peace and prosperity of the city to which I have carried you into exile" (NIV).

There was Mikhail, a former Spetsnaz, who'd seen things in Chechnya that made him jump at backfiring cars—Oksana, who'd fled her oligarch husband with nothing but her daughter and a suitcase. Dmitri, gay, Georgian, doubly exiled, sitting in the back row like me, trying to be invisible in a room where everyone was visible to God.

The pastor, Father Nikolai (Orthodox turned evangelical, long story), preached with his whole body. Arms waving, voice rising and falling like the Moscow Metro. I understood maybe every tenth word, but I understood everything.

You want to know what saved me? Tuesday nights at Natalya's apartment. She taught English to survive, but taught the Bible to live. Eight women crammed around her kitchen table, including Chen's cousin, who'd fled China, and Anastasia, who'd escaped an abusive marriage in Belarus.

Natalya's apartment: 400 square feet in Sham Shui Po, the non-glamorous part of Hong Kong. Kitchen table from a street market, wobbled unless you wedged paper under one leg. Mismatched chairs that told stories: one from an office closure, one from a restaurant that went under, one that looked like it escaped from a grandmother's estate sale.

Tea served in glasses, not cups, because "cups are for coffee, glasses are for tea, this is civilization." Sugar cubes that had absorbed Hong Kong humidity and stuck together like sweet concrete. Cookies that were more idea than substance but shared with love that was substantial.

"In Russia," Natalya would say, "we have saying: 'The same boiling water that hardens the egg softens the carrot.' Suffering doesn't make you better or worse. Reveals what you already are."

She had this way of laughing that made you feel like maybe your mistakes weren't fatal. Maybe your failures weren't final.

Her laugh started as a wheeze, like an accordion with asthma, then exploded into something between a cackle and a hymn. Contagious. You couldn't not laugh when Natalya laughed. She'd slap the table, tea glasses jumping, everyone grabbing their drinks before they spilled.

"You Americans," she'd say, wiping tears, "you think God is vending machine. Put in prayer, get out blessing. But God is more like... how you say... that casino game?"

"Slot machine?"

"No! The one with cards."

"Poker?"

"Yes! God is poker player. Sometimes He folds, sometimes He raises, but He never shows His cards until the end."

March 2015. Natalya introduced me to Stefaniya at a church potluck. Ukrainian. Beautiful. But more than that, she understood complicated journeys.

The potluck was chaos. Russians brought salads that were ninety percent mayonnaise. Ukrainians brought varenyky that looked like edible pillows. Kazakhs brought horse sausage, which I pretended to enjoy. I brought KFC because I panicked, and it was the only thing I could think of.

Stefaniya was wearing a dress the color of sunflowers, appropriate since she was Ukrainian. She was laughing at my KFC contribution, not mean laughing, but delighted laughing, like I'd solved a problem nobody knew existed.

"Everyone here is running from something," Stefaniya said, gesturing at the fellowship hall full of Russians, Ukrainians, Kazakhs, and one lost Texan. "But maybe we're all running to something too."

"What are you running from?" I asked.

"The idea that home is a place instead of a person." She smiled. "What about you?"

"The idea that broken things can't be beautiful."

She had a scar on her left hand, curved like a crescent moon. "Bread knife," she said when she caught me looking. "I was twelve, helping babusya, not paying attention. Twenty stitches. She cried more than I did."

I showed her my scar, the one on my palm from punching a window after the accident. "Stupidity," I said. "And Jack Daniel's."

"We match," she said, and somehow that felt like a proposal.

Nine months later, we married at the courthouse. Simple ceremony. Viktor was my witness, standing where my father would have stood if pride hadn't built walls between us. The entire Slavic church came to the reception, bringing dishes I couldn't pronounce but tasted like belonging.

The Geography of Grace

Brother Martinez found me at a Dallas conference in 2018. Found is the right word; I was hiding in the hotel breakfast area at 5 AM, avoiding the crowds.

The Hilton Anatole, the one with the weird art collection. I was sitting by the window overlooking the sculpture garden, eating runny eggs and burnt bacon, reading my phone and pretending to be busy. Standard conference avoidance behavior.

Martinez just appeared, like ministers do. Six-foot-two, tattoos crawling up his neck like ivy made of ink, wearing a suit that didn't quite hide his past. "You're the guy," he said, pointing with a hand that had JESÚS tattooed on the knuckles. "The one who traveled everywhere looking for God."

"How'd you know?"

"Brother, your testimony reads like a travel blog with a theology degree. Singapore, Shanghai, Jerusalem, man, I found God in cell block D. You learned from believers worldwide. I learned from a lifer named Tito who couldn't read but had memorized half the Bible."

He sat down uninvited, the way people do when they recognize pain.

Stole my bacon, too. Just reached over and took it, like we were old friends. "Vegetarian now," he said, eating my bacon. "Except for bacon. God understands."

"Tell me about Tito," I said.

"Twenty-five to life. Killed a man in a bar fight. Couldn't read when he went in. Other inmates taught him using the Bible, the only book they had enough copies of. By year ten, he could quote whole chapters. By year fifteen, he was teaching theology to seminary students who visited."

"Is he still..."

"He died last year. COVID," Martinez said, pulling out his phone to show me a video. "They held a memorial inside the prison yard. Hundreds of inmates standing quiet. Even the guards looked shaken. The warden gave the eulogy."

The video was shaky, probably filmed on a contraband phone. You could see the prison chapel, cinder blocks painted beige, a cross made from welded rebar. The warden, a white guy who looked like every cop show captain ever, crying actual tears, saying, "Tito made me believe in redemption."

Martinez leaned forward. "You logged enough miles to circle the globe looking for faith. Tito found it in a six-by-eight cell. Same God, hermano. Just different classrooms."

He was right. From Kunsan, South Korea, where I'd vacationed as a kid, to Abu Dhabi boardrooms, from Portsmouth shipyards to South American petroleum projects, I'd searched the world for what Tito found in prison. What Chen's grandmother found in suffering. What Yusuf found in forgiveness. What Maria found in pixels. What my Slavic family found in exile.

What I Learned (The Time-Saving Edition)

Listen, I could have saved two decades if I'd learned these lessons earlier. So let me save you some time:

From Singapore: Success without soul is just expensive failure. If James hadn't shared his grief over Tiger beer, I'd probably be on my fourth divorce, still circling bigger numbers on bar napkins.

From Shanghai: When they take everything, become what they can't take. Chen's grandmother became a living Bible. Three years in prison taught her what three decades of freedom couldn't: faith isn't something you have. It's something you are.

183

From Jerusalem: Forgiveness is a daily decision, not a one-time feeling. Every morning, choose coffee over poison. Yusuf's fifteen-minute lesson saved me from forty years of bitterness.

From Rio: The Church is bigger than your building, broader than your bandwidth. Maria's digital ministry prepared me for 2020 when every church went online overnight. One conversation with her saved our congregation when COVID hit.

From Hong Kong: Family isn't always blood. Sometimes it's Russians and Ukrainians who pray for you in languages you don't understand, but your heart does. Two years in that church taught me more about belonging than forty years in America.

From prison, via Martinez: God lives in places we'd never look. Tito's cell block congregation included murderers, thieves, and one guy who embezzled from a church. They all found grace in the least graceful place on earth. If God can work in supermax, He can work in your situation.

Your Coordinates in God's Global Story

Right now, as you read this:

- Chen's grandmother's songs are still being sung in Shanghai house churches
- Yusuf is brewing coffee and choosing blessing in Jerusalem
- Maria's digital disciples span six continents (her successor texts me their testimonies)
- Viktor shares his mother's bread with new foreigners in Hong Kong
- Brother Martinez tells inmates that cells can't contain grace

And somewhere, in ways you can't see yet, your story is connected to theirs.

Last week, Alex asked why we pray for "all those people with weird names."

"Because they saved Daddy's life," I told him.

"Were you drowning?"

"Yeah, buddy. In a different kind of water."

Evan, leaning in the doorway and pretending to play with his phone, said, "Can they pray for us too? Sometimes we need saving."

Out of the mouths of babes and teenagers pretending not to care.

Welcome to the family. We've been waiting for you.

CHAPTER NINE

Gratitude as a Weapon

Finding Joy and Strength in Daily Thankfulness

The turbulence hit somewhere over the Pacific, 35,000 feet above nothing but dark water and whatever mysteries the ocean keeps. But this wasn't the kind of turbulence that makes you grip your armrest or reconsider your atheism. This was different, the soul-shaking kind that happens when you realize you're running from something that's inside you, and no amount of altitude or distance is going to help.

Singapore Airlines flight SQ890, Hong Kong to San Francisco. Seat 23C because I'm too cheap for business class but too old for a middle seat in the back. It was one of those Airbus A350s that supposedly have better air pressure, the kind that promise you won't feel like death warmed over when you land. Still felt like death. Some things technology can't fix.

I'd just left Stefaniya in our cramped Kowloon apartment. Eight months married, and here I was flying away. Again. The irony wasn't lost on me; my second marriage ended precisely because of flights like this one. Too many hotels where the sheets smelled like industrial bleach. Too many "sorry, honey, I'll be home next week" phone calls that turned into "actually, maybe the week after." Too many missed dinners, missed moments, missed chances to be present.

The guy next to me, a Chinese businessman in a suit that probably cost more than my first car, was already snoring, that particular kind of airplane sleep that looks uncomfortable but apparently works. Three rows back, a baby had opinions about air travel that they were sharing with everyone. My lower back was staging its usual protest against airplane seats designed by someone who apparently hated the human spine.

The businessman's watch was a Patek Philippe. I knew because he kept checking it before he passed out, like time was supposed to move differently at 35,000 feet. His briefcase, a genuine Louis Vuitton—not the Canal Street special—was tucked precisely under his seat. Even his snoring sounded expensive, like he'd practiced it at a Swiss finishing school.

The baby, though. That kid had lungs. The kind of cry that starts as a whimper and builds to something that could shatter wine glasses. The mother, maybe twenty-five, was doing that bounce-walk in the aisle that all parents learn, that specific rhythm that sometimes works and sometimes makes you feel like you're trying.

The flight attendant served what they optimistically called dinner. Some kind of chicken (I think) with rice that had given up on life somewhere over Guam. As I stared at this sad meal, something broke loose inside me. Maybe it was exhaustion. I'd been running on three hours of sleep and airport coffee. Perhaps it was God tapping me on the shoulder with His cosmic two-by-four. But right there, seat 23C, instead of opening my laptop to review the contracts that were the whole reason for this trip, I found myself typing something else entirely:

"Things I'm grateful for today."

The laptop was my old ThinkPad, the one with three dead pixels and a space bar that stuck if you didn't hit it just right. I'd been carrying it for five years, through seventeen countries, and it had more airline miles than most pilots. The Word document was titled "Contract_Review_Project_FINAL" but I deleted all that and just started typing.

The cursor blinked at me, waiting. Accusing. What exactly was I grateful for? I was flying away from my new wife to close a deal I didn't care about for money we needed but wouldn't make us happy. I was repeating patterns that had already destroyed one marriage. I was 43 years old and still hadn't learned how to stay still.

But then I started typing:

"Stefaniya's laugh when I butchered the Russian word for 'good morning', 'Доброе утро', came out sounding like I was gargling vodka."

She'd actually snorted coffee through her nose when I said it. Real coffee, not that instant stuff, because even in our tiny apartment with one burner that worked and another that sometimes worked, she insisted on real coffee. "Life is too short for bad coffee," she'd say in that accent that made everything sound like poetry. The coffee came out of her nose, and she laughed so hard she couldn't breathe, and I thought, "This is it. This is what love sounds like."

"The note she hid in my suitcase that I found at security almost made me cry in front of TSA."

The note was on a Post-it, the yellow kind, stuck inside my passport. Her handwriting, that careful Cyrillic-trained script that made English letters look like art: "Come back to me. I choose you every day." The TSA agent, this huge guy with hands like ham hocks, saw me getting emotional and said, "First time leaving the wife?" I nodded. "Gets easier," he said. "But that's not always a good thing."

189

"A job that pays the bills even if it's eating my soul."

"This uncomfortable seat taking me toward provision for our future."

Simple? Yes. Profound? Hardly. But something shifted. Like adjusting the lens on a camera and suddenly everything comes into focus.

When Gratitude Becomes Warfare

My aunt, the one who basically raised me during summers when my parents needed a break, used to say: "Simon, you can count your troubles or count your blessings, but you can't do both at the same time. Your brain's not big enough, and frankly, neither is mine."

Aunt Gee ran Gee's Beauty Shop out of a converted garage in Stephenville, Texas. The sign out front was hand-painted, the 'G' in Gee starting to fade, so it looked like " ee's Beauty Shop." She'd do hair Tuesday through Saturday, closed Sunday for Jesus and Monday for sanity. The garage still smelled like motor oil under all the perm solution and Aqua Net.

Sunday mornings, though, you'd find her in the kitchen making biscuits and gravy from scratch. Flour dusted everything: the counters, her apron, and even her glasses, which were held together with a tiny piece of Scotch tape on the left side. She'd stir the gravy smooth from pan drippings, flour, and milk while gospel music played from a radio held together with duct tape. The biscuits came out perfect every time, fluffy inside, golden outside, good enough to make you believe in something bigger than yourself.

She was a beautician who built her business with grit and persistence, a wife who stood beside her husband as he carved out a career in real estate. She poured her life into serving people, listening to their stories in her chair. And still she sang while she cooked. Not because life was simple, but because gratitude was her rebellion against despair.

The key change here is creating a clear scene transition from the beauty shop to Sunday morning in her kitchen, eliminating the confusing repetition while keeping every precious detail. Now it reads like a single continuous memory rather than two drafts accidentally merged.

The radio was tuned to KSTV-FM 93.1, which usually played country, but on Sunday mornings, it became 'Nothing but the Good News,' and the familiar voice of the host filled the room with gospel music. Every third song was "I'll Fly Away" or some version of it. Uncle Runt, the one who made good in real estate, would come home for lunch, still in his one good suit that he wore to show houses, and they'd eat biscuits with butter and honey while Mahalia Jackson promised better days ahead.

They never had kids. Three miscarriages, then the doctor said, "Stop trying." I found this out when I was thirty, after my first divorce. Aunt Gee told me, while cutting my hair in that same garage-salon, her hands steady even while talking about the babies that never made it. "Some gardens don't grow what you plant," she said. "So, you tend what does grow, like you, kiddo."

I'd spent decades keeping score of what went wrong. That night in the Caribbean when everything changed, check. Two marriages that crumbled like stale bread, check and check. Parents whose fights echoed through my childhood, check. Business ventures that failed spectacularly, check, check, check. I was a professional grievance collector, curator of my own museum of mistakes.

But that night on the plane, typing on my laptop while the Pacific Ocean rolled by invisible beneath us, I started a different kind of collection.

When King David Knew What Neuroscientists Would Discover

Three weeks after that flight, I was sitting in our tiny Hong Kong apartment at 5 AM, jet-lagged and restless. Kowloon was waking up I could hear the first trains starting their runs, the convenience store downstairs rolling up its metal gate. I grabbed my Bible, the one with coffee stains on most pages and entire books falling out from overuse.

The convenience store was a 7-Eleven, of course. The owner, Mr. Liu, had this routine: gate up at 5:15, coffee brewing by 5:20, first customer (usually me) by 5:30. He'd nod, I'd nod, universal language of "too early for actual words." His coffee was terrible, bitter, and burnt, but it was there and it was hot, and sometimes that's all you need.

The Bible was NIV, bought at that Christian bookstore in Causeway Bay that was really just a corner of a bigger bookstore, like faith needing to rent space from commerce. The binding was held together with packing tape. Genesis was missing the first twenty pages. Revelation was coffee-stained beyond recognition. But Psalms was intact, probably because I'd reinforced it with clear tape like it was evidence in a crime scene.

Psalm 103 fell open (probably because that's where the binding was most broken): "Praise the Lord, my soul, and forget not all his benefits" (Psalm 103:2, NIV).

Forget not. Not "remember if convenient" or "recall when feeling spiritual." Forget not. It's a command, urgent, like someone grabbing you by the shoulders and shaking you awake.

David wasn't writing feel-good poetry from a palace. He wrote many psalms while running from Saul, sleeping in caves, wondering if each dawn would be his last. He knew what we're just discovering with our MRIs and neuroscience, that gratitude literally rewires your brain, creates new neural pathways, and changes the physical structure of how you think.

I looked this up later because I'm that guy who needs science to back up faith. Dr. Robert Emmons's foundational research demonstrated that gratitude practices, like journaling, are linked to better health and lower stress levels (Emmons & McCullough, 2003). Subsequent brain imaging studies by other researchers have provided a neurological explanation, revealing that feelings of gratitude activate the hypothalamus, a brain region that regulates stress, sleep, and metabolism (Zahn et al., 2009). Also, the medial prefrontal cortex lights up, the area associated with moral cognition and value judgment.

David didn't have fMRI machines. He had a harp, a bunch of sheep, and a king trying to kill him. But somehow, hiding in the Cave of Adullam with 400 other outlaws and losers, he figured out that gratitude wasn't about your circumstances. It was about your survival.

"Forget not ALL his benefits," David wrote. All. Not just the obvious ones. Not just the Instagram-worthy blessings. All of it. The cave that keeps you hidden. The outlaws who become your army. The wife who sneaks you food even though her father wants you dead. All of it counts.

But David didn't need peer-reviewed journals. He had caves,

enemies, and a God who showed up anyway. He knew gratitude wasn't positive thinking. It was survival equipment.

Building the Habit When Your Foundation's Already Cracked

Here's the thing about starting a gratitude practice when your life's falling apart: it feels like trying to paint a house that's on fire. Pointless. Maybe even insulting to the magnitude of your problems.

I tried those gratitude apps first. Downloaded seven of them. "Three Good Things," "The 5 Minute Journal," "Gratitude: Self-Care Journal," a bunch of others with names that sounded like wellness consultants. Each one wanted to send notifications: "Time to be grateful!" at 8 AM, when I was already late for work; at noon, when I was in meetings; and at 8 PM, when I just wanted to drink beer and pretend everything was fine.

Deleted them all after a week. Nothing says "you're failing at gratitude" like seventeen unacknowledged notifications asking what you're thankful for.

I started with index cards because my phone was too dangerous, too easy to spiral from gratitude app to email to news to existential crisis. Old school three-by-five cards from the Japan Home Centre in Causeway Bay. HK$12 for a pack of 100. The cashier looked at me like I was buying ancient technology, which I guess I was.

Every morning, before the Hong Kong trains started their assault on peace, before the emails began their daily invasion, I'd write three things.

Good days looked like:

- "Stefaniya said yes when this broken man proposed."

- "Found that incredible ramen place near Times Square where the owner remembers my order."

- "My parents are still alive; we might reconcile someday."

The ramen place was actually just a stall in a food court. Still, Mr. Tanaka (probably not his real name, but that's what he told me) would see me coming and start making my order: shoyu ramen, extra chashu, soft-boiled egg, no bamboo shoots because I'm apparently the only person in Asia who hates bamboo shoots. "Bamboo man!" he'd call out. That's what he called me. Bamboo man, because I didn't want bamboo. Hong Kong humor.

Hard days? Different story:

- "Coffee exists"

- "Made it through another night without nightmares about the accident"

- "The shower has hot water"

The shower thing wasn't a given. Our water heater was this ancient gas-powered thing that looked like it might explode every time you turned it on. You had to light the pilot with a match, yes, a match, reaching your hand into this metal box while gas hissed at you like an angry snake. Half the time it didn't light. Quarter of the time it lit then went out mid-shower. But that remaining quarter when it worked? Paradise.

Some days, that third one was a struggle. I'd sit there, pen hovering over the card, trying to find one more thing. Sometimes it was just "This pen works," or "I can see," or "My heart is still beating."

Once, I wrote "The cockroach is on his side of the apartment" because we'd developed a détente with this massive roach that lived behind our refrigerator. We called him Gerald. As long as Gerald stayed on his side, we coexisted. It's not much of a gratitude, but at 5 AM when you're trying to find thing number three, you take what you can get.

The point wasn't the profundity of what I wrote. The point was the practice of looking for light when darkness felt total.

The Contagion Effect

Six months into this practice, Stefaniya found me at our tiny kitchen table, really just a card table we'd bought from another expat who was leaving, with my cards spread out like some gratitude tarot reading. She picked one up, read it, and started crying.

The table was from an Australian couple who were moving back to Melbourne. Sixty Hong Kong dollars and IKEA's finest particleboard engineering. It wobbled unless you put a beer coaster under the back left leg. We had a collection of coasters from bars we couldn't afford just for table management.

Stefaniya was wearing my old Texas A&M t-shirt, the one with holes in both armpits, and her hair was doing that thing where it looked like she'd been electrocuted but somehow beautiful. That's love, when bedhead looks like a halo.

The card said: "Grateful that God gave me someone who sees past my past."

She looked at me, tears making tracks through her morning makeup, and said in her beautifully broken English, "You know what? I start too."

Her English in 2015 was enthusiastic but chaotic. She'd learned British English in Ukraine, then American English from movies, then Hong Kong English from the streets. It came out like linguistic jazz; you never knew what accent was coming next. "I start too" sounded like "I shtart tyoo" with this mix of Slavic and British that made my heart do stupid things.

That's when I learned gratitude is contagious. More contagious than complaint, though complaint spreads pretty fast too. But gratitude? It's like a virus that actually makes people healthier.

She started her own cards. At first in Ukrainian, then sometimes in Russian—her mother's parents spoke Ukrainian, her father's parents spoke Russian—so her thoughts moved easily between both. As her comfort with English grew, she began mixing all three. I'd find the cards tucked in random places, between books, in the silverware drawer, once in the freezer (still have no idea how that happened). Little testimonies to grace: "Simon tried to cook борщ," "Baby kicked today," "Found apartment with more than one room."

The борщ incident: I'd watched three YouTube videos, bought $200 HKD worth of vegetables, and spent four hours creating what can only be described as purple water with floating things. Stefaniya took one sip, said "Is... interesting," then ordered pizza. But she ate a whole bowl of my purple water first, because love means pretending your husband's cooking is edible.

The baby's kicking was our first pregnancy that made it past the first trimester. After two miscarriages, every kick felt like a miracle telegram from God saying, "Still here, still growing, still coming."

The 2020 Unraveling (And What Saved Us)

March 2020. Remember that? The world shut down like God hit the pause button. We were living in Texas by then, and had our first child, another on the way. I watched grown men fight over toilet paper at HEB. Churches went dark overnight. Schools became kitchen tables. The whole world held its breath, wondering if this was how it all ended.

March 13, 2020, specifically. Friday the 13th, because of course it was. I was at the HEB on Interstate 45 when they announced the lockdown. This guy in a Cowboys jersey literally grabbed the last pack of Charmin Ultra from an elderly woman's cart. She just stood there, holding her cart handle, looking like she'd witnessed the collapse of civilization. Which I guess she had. I gave her the pack from my cart. Not because I'm noble, I just figured if this was the apocalypse, I didn't want 'toilet paper thief enabler' on my eternal resume.

I drove home with one pack of toilet paper and the growing realization that everything was about to change.

Within days, our eighteen hundred and fifty square feet shrank. What once felt perfectly adequate became a cage we decorated with Amazon boxes and anxiety. Alex was thirteen months old then, too young to understand why his world had shifted. No more daycare faces. No more routine. Just Mommy and Daddy trying to pretend everything was normal while the news played pandemic death counts like sports scores. I spent hours in the garage on Zoom calls for work, my voice echoing off concrete walls while Alex pressed his tiny hands against the door, confused why Daddy was talking to a laptop instead of him.

Stefaniya was seven months pregnant, exhausted, and terrified of giving birth during a plague. Every night at 2 AM, I'd find her scrolling through 'COVID pregnancy complications until I had to hide her phone on the highest shelf in the pantry, behind the emergency beans we'd never eat.

Then in April, death found us anyway, not through COVID, but through time.

Stefaniya's babushka passed in Ukraine. The woman who survived Stalin's purges, Hitler's invasion, Chernobyl's radiation, and post-Soviet collapse died quietly in the village home her husband built with his own hands. COVID protocols meant no hospital. Border closures meant no funeral. We couldn't even send flowers.

Stefaniya cried in the shower so Alex wouldn't see. I sat in my garage prayer corner, trying to practice gratitude like the devotional books said, writing 'healthy family' and 'food in pantry' in my journal. At the same time, my wife grieved a grandmother our children would never meet. That's when I learned gratitude isn't about feeling thankful. Sometimes it's just refusing to let despair win, even when it has every right to.

Babushka Oksana, 94 years old, 4 feet 10 inches of Ukrainian titanium. She'd hidden Jews during the war, sold everything she owned to buy antibiotics on the black market when Stefaniya's mother got tuberculosis, and walked seventeen kilometers to church every Sunday until she was 91. She died in her sleep, in the bed where she'd given birth to all four of her children, in the house that still didn't have indoor plumbing but had icons in every corner.

The funeral was on Viber. Nine people gathered around a phone propped against a hymnal, livestreaming goodbye. The priest's voice kept cutting out. Someone's rooster crowed during the prayer. The connection dropped right as they lowered the casket. Technology is failing us when we need it most.

Stefaniya didn't leave our bedroom for three days. I brought her tea, black tea with too much sugar, the way Babushka made it, held her while she cried, and ran out of words by day two. What do you say when someone loses their anchor and can't even say goodbye properly?

She'd lie there watching Ukrainian YouTube videos of her grandmother's village, these shaky phone recordings of nothing, chickens pecking, wind through sunflowers, old women selling vegetables at the market. "I can't remember her voice exactly," she said on day three. "I know the words she would say, but the exact sound is leaving."

That's when gratitude became a weapon instead of a wellness trend. Not gratitude for the situation, that would be obscene. But gratitude in the situation.

I found myself in 2 Samuel 22:29: "You, Lord, are my lamp; the Lord turns my darkness into light" (NIV). Not "removes my darkness." Not "prevents darkness." Turns it into light. There's alchemy in that promise.

So, our family practice evolved. At dinner, even when dinner was cereal because we were too exhausted to cook, we'd go around the table:

"Where did you see God show up today, even in something tiny?" "What hard thing taught you something?" "Who showed you kindness when you didn't deserve it?"

Alex's answers were poetry disguised as toddler rambling: "God showed up in the ant that carried a crumb bigger than himself." "Being sad about babushka taught me that love doesn't stop when people do." "Mama gave me goldfish crackers even though I drew on the wall."

That last one, he'd taken a Sharpie to our dining room wall, drawn what he insisted was a portrait of our family but looked more like potatoes with stick legs. Stefaniya was too exhausted to discipline. Just handed him goldfish and said, "At least you gave Daddy hair."

Alex was only thirteen months old. He couldn't speak yet, not really. But the day he saw me crying, he toddled over and touched the tears on my cheek with his tiny hand, like he was trying to understand where they came from. And in that moment, I realized something a toddler couldn't put into words: tears aren't weakness. They're proof that the heart still works.

I had to excuse myself from the table. Went to the garage, my prayer closet, and cried my own grateful tears.

The Science and the Sacred

The research is everywhere now. Gratitude increases dopamine and serotonin, the same neurotransmitters targeted by antidepressants. It activates the hypothalamus, regulating stress. It triggers the ventral tegmental area, producing feelings of long-term contentment.

I went deep into the research during lockdown because, honestly, what else was there to do? I read every study I could get my hands on. Dr. Martin Seligman at the University of Pennsylvania found that writing and delivering a single gratitude letter can create a lasting lift in happiness, a 2005 study he later discussed in *Flourish* (2011).

Then there was Dr. Sonja Lyubomirsky at UC Riverside, whose work surprised me even more. She found that gratitude journaling only once or twice a week often works better than doing it every day (Lyubomirsky, 2007). Something about avoiding that mental drift where blessings become background noise.

The one that got me was a study from Indiana University. They had people recovering from anxiety and depression write gratitude letters. Three months later, their brains showed greater neural sensitivity in the medial prefrontal cortex, the learn-to-be-grateful part of the brain. The brain literally rewired itself. Neuroplasticity in action, synapses firing new patterns, dendrites reaching toward hope instead of despair.

But knowing the science doesn't make the practice easier. It's like knowing exercise is good for you while being pinned to your couch by depression. The gap between knowledge and action feels infinite.

What bridged that gap for me wasn't willpower. It was worship. Not necessarily the singing kind, though that helps too. But the recognition that gratitude is worship. It's saying to God, "Even in this mess, I see You. Even in this pain, I acknowledge You. Even when I don't understand, I trust You."

I started treating my gratitude cards like prayers. Each morning, before writing, I'd hold the blank card and think, "This is my offering." Like the widow's mite, not much, but all I had. Some mornings, writing "coffee exists" felt like as much of a sacrifice of praise as David dancing before the ark.

Actually, started dating them like historical documents. March 27, 2020 - Day 14 of lockdown. Grateful for: 1) Stefaniya hasn't killed me yet despite being trapped together 24/7, 2) Alex only threw his sippy cup at my head twice today instead of the usual seven times, 3) Found one last package of diapers hidden behind the paper towels at Target.

Looking back at those cards now is like reading dispatches from a war zone.

Gratitude in the Valley of the Shadow

Let me be brutally honest: gratitude isn't spiritual Prozac. It doesn't erase trauma. The man who died in the Caribbean didn't come back because I wrote thank-you cards to God. My divorces didn't unhappen because I counted my blessings. My parents' marriage didn't heal retroactively because I practiced appreciation.

He's still gone. A life ended too soon. People who loved him still carry a quiet ache that never fully leaves. There are empty chairs at tables that should have held laughter. No amount of gratitude changes that reality. Some losses simply stay with you, softening maybe, but never erased.

My first marriage still crashed and burned in a spectacular fashion that involved lawyers, divided furniture, and two Golden Retrievers we never should have adopted in the first place. She picked them out while I was overseas so she wouldn't feel alone, but the truth was I was gone too much to be any real caretaker, and she didn't want them once the novelty wore off. By the time everything fell apart, the dogs ended up at an animal shelter—collateral damage in a marriage that couldn't hold.

My second marriage still ended with me signing papers in a Hong Kong law office while Josephine was already on a plane back to Houston.

But here's what did happen: my perspective shifted. Not in a "everything happens for a reason" way that makes me want to punch people who say that. But in an "even in the worst things, there are glimpses of grace" way.

I'm grateful that hitting rock bottom taught me I can survive anything. I'm grateful my failed marriages showed me what love isn't, preparing me to recognize what it is. I'm grateful that starting over at 40 meant I had enough scars to appreciate gentleness when God brought Stefaniya into my life. I'm grateful my parents' struggles made me fight harder for my own family.

Specific gratitude from the dark times:

- Grateful for the bartender at The Dublin Jack in Hong Kong who called me a taxi when I couldn't stand, probably saved my life

- Grateful for the lawyer who said, "You need therapy more than you need a divorce attorney" (I got both)

- Grateful for rock bottom because at least it's solid ground

- Grateful for the miscarriages because they taught us to treasure the pregnancies that survived

- Grateful for poverty because it taught us the difference between want and need

- Grateful for betrayal because it taught me the value of loyalty

Dark? Maybe. Honest? Absolutely. And honesty, I've learned, is where healing starts.

Making It Real in Your Real Life

Look, I get it. You're drowning in responsibilities. Your marriage needs CPR. Your kids think screens are a food group. Your job is slowly killing you. The last thing you need is another self-help checklist from someone pretending their life is perfect.

So, let's make this stupid simple and actually doable:

The Morning Three (Phone-Free Zone) Keep a notebook by your bed. Not your phone, that's a portal to anxiety. An actual notebook. Before your feet hit the floor, before the day's demands start their assault, write three things. Don't overthink it. Yesterday mine were:

1. "Stefaniya still chooses me after 10 years."

2. "Coffee exists" (this makes the list a lot)

3. "My back hurts less than yesterday."

The notebook is a composition book from Walmart, $0.97. The pen is whatever I stole from a hotel. The handwriting looks like a doctor having a seizure. Doesn't matter. God reads chicken scratch.

The Dinner Table Check-In: Everyone shares one good thing. Non-negotiable. Yes, even your teenager who communicates exclusively in grunts and eye rolls. We've had nights where the "good thing" was "dinner's over" or "tomorrow isn't today." That counts.

Last Tuesday, Evan (our four-year-old) said his good thing was "Daddy didn't make us eat his cooking." Stefaniya laughed so hard she cried. Alex added, "My good thing is Mama crying happy instead of sad." Even Olivia, our baby girl who's just learning to talk, said "Good doggy!" even though we don't have a dog. We counted it.

The Voice Memo Hack: Houston traffic is a special kind of hell. Instead of using that time to rehearse arguments with people who aren't there, record gratitude. Voice memo to yourself. "Grateful for AC in Texas summer. Grateful for this podcast. Grateful I'm not on the motorcycle behind me in this heat." Send them to yourself. On dark days, listening to your own voice recounting grace is medicine.

My voice memos are comedy gold. Half of them have me screaming at someone who cut me off, then immediately saying, "Grateful that person didn't cause an accident. Grateful for brakes. Grateful I didn't actually ram them even though I wanted to." It's gratitude with a side of road rage—very Houston.

The Photo Practice: One picture daily of something you're grateful for. Not for Instagram, this isn't performance. For you. My phone's full of random stuff: Stefaniya's coffee mug with lipstick marks, my son's Lego creation that looks nothing like what he says it is, sunrise over I-10, my daughter's hand holding mine. It's become a visual psalm, a gallery of grace.

Current phone storage: 47,293 photos. At least 10,000 are gratitude shots. Weird stuff like:

• The spider in our bathroom, I'm grateful, doesn't pay rent but kills mosquitoes

• My truck at 267,000 miles, still running

• The dent in the garage wall from when I taught Alex to ride a bike

• Stefaniya asleep on the couch at 7 PM because three kids are exhausting

• The burn mark on our kitchen counter from when I learned that not all pots have heat-resistant handles

The Time-Saving Mathematics of Thankfulness

Here's what gratitude actually saves you:

Comparison Scrolling: Time wasted: 2+ hours daily on social media envy. Gratitude alternative: 5-minute morning list. Time saved: 115 minutes daily

I tracked this. Used that Screen Time feature that makes you hate yourself. Average daily Instagram usage: 2 hours 34 minutes. Looking at what? People's fake happy lives, ads for things I don't need, and videos of cats. Switched to gratitude cards. Now Instagram gets 20 minutes max, usually while on the toilet. TMI? Everything important happens in bathrooms, in prayers, in tears, and, apparently, in gratitude epiphanies.

Worry Spirals: Time wasted: 3-4 hours of "what if" thinking. Gratitude alternative: Evening review of God's faithfulness. Time saved: Mental energy redirected to actual problem-solving

Resentment Rehearsals: Time wasted: Endless mental arguments with people who hurt you. Gratitude alternative: Praying a blessing over difficult people. Time saved: Emotional bandwidth for present relationships

The bottom line: My gratitude practice takes 10 minutes daily but saves me hours of mental and emotional drain. That's kingdom economics: small investment, massive return.

YOUR NEXT STEP

Tomorrow morning, before touching your phone, before the day starts its demands, write three things you're grateful for. Don't overthink. Don't try to be profound. Mine this morning were: 'Woke up,' 'Indoor plumbing,' and 'Kids still think I'm funny.'

Actually, let me be specific about this morning, September 21, 2022:

1. 'Woke up without the alarm because Olivia yelled DADA DADA DADA at 5:47 AM while shaking her crib rails like a tiny prisoner.'

2.   'Indoor plumbing that only requires one handle turn, not a pilot light and prayer.'

3.   'Kids still laugh at my dad's jokes even though they're terrible.'

Example of said dad joke: 'Why don't scientists trust atoms? Because they make up everything!' Alex groaned like I'd personally offended him. Evan laughed hysterically because at four, anything with the word 'everything' is comedy gold, then asked me to tell it again seventeen times. Olivia banged her sippy cup on her highchair tray because everyone else was making noise. Stefaniya said something in Ukrainian that definitely wasn't complimentary. But they all smiled. That's a win.

Start there. Build from there. Watch what grows.

Because here's what I've learned flying over oceans, building businesses, destroying marriages, and finally finding grace: Gratitude isn't about having a perfect life. It's about finding a perfect God in your imperfect mess. It's about saying 'thank You' even when you want to say, 'why me?' It's about choosing to count gifts instead of grievances.

This morning, while writing this, Alex came into my office (the garage) and said, 'Daddy, what are you grateful for right now?'

'That you asked that question,' I said.

'That's cheating,' he said. 'Pick something real.'

So I did: 'I'm grateful that God gave me a son who won't let me cheat at gratitude.'

He thought about it, then said, 'I'm grateful you're writing your book even though it makes you cry sometimes.'

Seven years old and already understanding that gratitude and grief can share the same space.

You're not just making a list. You're building a life. You're rewiring your brain. You're teaching your soul a new song. And that song? It's going to sustain you through storms you can't imagine yet.

Trust me. I'm singing it still.

CHAPTER TEN

God's Deeper Why

How Trials Reveal Your Calling and Refine Your Faith

It's been a long journey putting this book together. I was sitting in my home office in Texas, wrestling with this final chapter like Jacob with his angel, when my oldest came running in with tears streaming down his face. He'd fallen off his bike, nothing serious, thank God, just scraped knees and bruised pride, but watching his pain triggered something ancient in me.

Alex burst through the door at 4:37 PM on a Tuesday. I know the exact time because I'd been staring at the cursor blinking on my screen for seventeen minutes, trying to figure out how to end a book about finding God in the wreckage when some days I still feel lost in the debris. His Superman band-aids from the morning, he'd insisted on wearing them preventatively, had come unstuck and were flapping like tiny capes of failure.

The bike, a blue Huffy we'd bought at Walmart for his sixth birthday, was still lying in the driveway where he'd abandoned it. Training wheels removed just last week. He'd been so proud, wobbling down our cul-de-sac like a drunk businessman, but vertical and moving forward.

Some of us carry invisible injuries that ache when the weather changes. Mine tends to flare up when I see innocence collide with a world that doesn't always cushion our falls. My son's tears weren't just about skinned knees. They were about discovering that gravity is unforgiving, that concrete doesn't care about your feelings, that sometimes you can do everything right and still end up bleeding.

I held him while he sobbed, his small body shaking with the injustice of it all. "I was being careful!" he protested. "I was wearing my helmet! Why did I still fall?"

The helmet, a Paw Patrol one he's almost outgrown, had a new scratch across Marshall's face. $24.99 at Target, supposed to keep him safe. Did its job, I guess. His head was fine. But there's no helmet for the heart, no protection for that moment when you realize the world has edges and they're sharp.

His knee was bleeding through a hole in his jeans, the good ones Stefaniya had bought at Old Navy, now destined for the play clothes pile. Blood mixed with driveway dirt, creating that particular childhood paste of injury and earth.

Why indeed.

Like Leonard Cohen sang, "There is a crack in everything / That's how the light gets in." But when you're six years old with blood running down your shin, you don't want poetry. You want the pain to stop. You want to understand why being good didn't protect you from getting hurt.

When God's Plan Feels Like Punishment

You want to know what suffering really teaches you? It's not some grand theological lesson wrapped in a bow and delivered by angels. It's more like learning a new language, the language of loss, of questions without answers, of faith that sometimes feels as thin as tissue paper but somehow holds the weight of your entire existence.

I remember that on Thursday, August 17, 2023, in our small group, we met at this coffee shop on Montrose called 'Siphon.' Used to be a tattoo parlor in the 90s, still has exposed brick and pipes, and they painted it black to look industrial. The church is being renovated after that pipe burst in the youth room, and honestly, the coffee's better here anyway. They have this barista, college kid named Tyler from UH with gauges in his ears and a cross tattoo on his forearm, who makes a cortado that could convert atheists.

Marcus asked the question we all dance around: "If God loves us, why does He let us hurt so bad?"

Marcus Thompson, forty-three, sells insurance, drives a Toyota Camry with 180,000 miles, just lost his mother to Alzheimer's after a seven-year decline. He asked this while holding a coffee cup that said "But First, Coffee," like it was an anchor keeping him from floating away.

The group: eight men who meet every Thursday at 7 PM, except when the Cowboys play Thursday night, then we meet at 5:30. We've got Marcus, obviously. Jim, the contractor who's been sober for six years. Eduardo, who doesn't talk much but shows up every week. Mike from my old Miami group, who moved to Texas. Tom the widower. Brad, who's going through a divorce. Carl, whose son is in jail. And me, still carrying the weight of a Caribbean night.

The room went quiet. You could hear the espresso machine hissing, the barista calling out drinks with too many adjectives. Everyone found somewhere else to look. Bibles. Coffee cups. The fascinating wood grain of the reclaimed table.

I used to have neat answers for that question. Used to quote Romans 5:3-4 about suffering producing perseverance, character, and hope. Like it was spiritual algebra where pain was the variable and hope was the solution, but after you've walked through real darkness, not theoretical darkness, not metaphorical darkness, but the kind where you can't see your hand in front of your face, those verses hit different.

"I don't know," I said finally. "I don't know why God lets us hurt. But I know He hurts with us."

Marcus looked at me like I'd just admitted Santa wasn't real. "That's it? That's your answer? God hurts, too?"

He actually set his coffee down when he said this. Marcus never sets his coffee down. It's his security blanket, always in his hand, even when it's empty. But he set it down and stared at me with eyes that had watched his mother forget his name, letter by letter, memory by memory.

My throat tightened. I could feel everyone waiting, these broken men in a former tattoo parlor, hoping I had something better than platitudes.

"Yeah," I said. "Sometimes that's all we get. Emmanuel. God with us. Not God fixing us, not God explaining to us, just God with us."

Jim cleared his throat, that sound he makes when he's about to say something that matters. "My sponsor in AA says the same thing. 'I can't tell you why you became an alcoholic, but I can sit with you while you become sober.'"

Marcus picked up his coffee cup again. Held it with both hands. Nodded once. Sometimes that's all the theology we need."

Finding God in the Wreckage

The morning after my life changed forever in the Caribbean, I remember staring at the ceiling of my hotel room. The ceiling fan wobbled slightly, probably installed by someone who didn't care about perfect balance. The trade winds were blowing through the window, carrying the sounds of roosters and reggae, paradise continuing its soundtrack, while my world had gone silent.

The hotel wasn't memorable in any way except for that night. A basic roadside place with thin walls and a ceiling fan that spun just off-center. I remember the fan more than the room itself. Five blades. I counted them over and over, trying to quiet my mind. One blade had a crack running through it, a jagged line that looked like a lightning bolt when the shadows hit it, or a river, depending on the angle. Funny what details stay with you when the world has fallen apart.

The sheets smelled like that industrial detergent all hotels use, the kind that's supposed to smell like "ocean breeze," but really smells like chemicals pretending to be nature. There was a gecko on the wall, one of those translucent ones where you can see their organs. It hadn't moved in an hour. I envied its stillness.

All I could think about was a family somewhere on this island planning a funeral because of me. The authorities said I couldn't have stopped in time, physics being what it is. But knowing that didn't stop the mental replay. That sound. That moment when time dilated and a second felt like an hour, but still wasn't enough to change anything.

I grabbed the hotel Bible, you know, those Gideon ones with the thin pages that tear if you look at them wrong. It fell open to Matthew 11:28: "Come to me, all you who are weary and burdened, and I will give you rest" (NIV).

The Bible was placed by the Gideons in 1987, according to the stamp inside. Someone had underlined verses in pencil: John 3:16, obviously, Romans 8:28, and Psalm 23. Tourist verses. Verses for people passing through paradise, not for people whose paradise just became hell.

The pages were warped from humidity, giving Jesus's words a wavy quality, like they were underwater. Appropriate, since I was drowning.

I wanted to throw it across the room. Rest? I didn't deserve rest. Rest was for people who hadn't just ended someone's story. Rest was for people whose hands were clean, whose consciences were clear, whose sleep wasn't haunted by a face they'd seen for only seconds but would remember forever.

But here's the thing about grace: it shows up uninvited, especially when you think you deserve it least. Grace is like that friend who has a key to your house and lets themselves in when you're too depressed to answer the door.

The Purpose Hidden in Our Pain

My friend, let's call him Dr. Muli, because he hates when I use his real name in stories, who teaches at Dallas Theological Seminary, is a brilliant guy, has three PhDs, and reads Hebrew for fun, once told me over lunch at this mediocre Thai place that suffering is like a master sculptor's chisel.

There's this little Thai place I used to meet Dr. Muli at—one of those strip-mall restaurants with plastic plants, gold elephants on the wall, and a menu laminated so many times it could survive a hurricane. The pad thai cost under ten dollars and tasted like someone had learned the recipe from a five-minute tutorial online. Dr. Muli always ordered mild yellow curry. Three degrees on his wall, yet a single chili pepper defeated him every time.

He was wearing his teaching uniform: khakis that needed ironing, a blue Oxford shirt with a coffee stain on the pocket, and a tie that his wife clearly picked because it actually matched. His glasses, thick black frames that went out of style in 1987 and came back in 2015, kept sliding down as he got animated.

"Simon," he said, pushing his glasses up his nose the way he does when he's about to say something that'll mess with your head, "God isn't trying to hurt us. He's trying to reveal us. To show us who we really are beneath all the stuff we pile on top, the success, the image, the carefully curated social media presence."

I was skeptical. "So, God causes suffering to reveal our true selves?"

"No," he said, stealing a spring roll from my plate. "God doesn't cause suffering. We live in a broken world where broken things happen. But God doesn't waste suffering. He redeems it. Transforms it. Uses it to chip away everything that isn't essential until only what matters remains."

He drew on a napkin while talking, because professors can't help themselves. Drew a block of marble, then started making small marks to show pieces being chipped away. His illustration looked more like a deformed potato, but I got the point.

"Michelangelo said he didn't create David," Muli continued, rice falling from his chopsticks because he insists on using them despite having the dexterity of a bear in mittens. "He revealed David by removing everything that wasn't David. Maybe that's what God does with suffering. Removes everything that isn't really us."

When Your Trials Become Your Ministry

You know what nobody prepared me for? How my worst moments

would become my most powerful ministry tools. These days, when I'm talking with someone who's drowning in guilt or loss, I don't start with verses. I don't start with theological explanations. I start with "I know what it's like to carry something heavy."

That Sunday in March, March 10, 2024, a young guy named Trevor came up after service. Twenty-eight years old, works at Wells Fargo, wearing a suit that was trying too hard because he'd come straight from work, even though banks don't open on Sundays, probably had been sitting in his car in the parking lot, working up the courage to come in.

The parking lot at The Fellowship Church, the one they just repaved because the potholes were becoming lawsuit risks. Texas sun at 12:47 PM, the kind of November heat that makes you question global warming deniers. Cars leaving around us, the after-church exodus to Chili's and Olive Garden, the Protestant pilgrimage to unlimited breadsticks.

His wife had miscarried their first child two weeks ago. He stood there in that heat, sweat running down his face or maybe tears, hard to tell in that brightness, and asked how God could let this happen.

"We did everything right," he said, voice cracking. "We waited until marriage. We prayed for this baby. We bought the crib, spent $400 at Buy Buy Baby, more than we could afford. Painted the nursery yellow because we wanted to be surprised. How could God give us this gift and then take it away?"

His hands kept moving while he talked, pulling at his wedding ring, adjusting his tie, checking his phone like maybe his wife had texted that it was all a mistake, the baby was fine. She hadn't. She was probably at home, in that yellow nursery, trying to decide whether to leave it yellow or paint it back to beige.

Twenty years ago, I would have quoted Romans 8:28 at him. Ten years ago, I might have shared my own story to show him pain could have purpose. But now? Now I just stood with him in that heat and said, "I don't know why. But I know what it's like when God feels cruel and grace feels like a lie. And I know, not believe, not hope, but know, that somehow, impossibly, you'll survive this."

He started crying then. Real tears, not Texas-sun-in-your-eyes tears. His shoulders shook like Alex's had with his skinned knee, that same discovery that the world has edges and sometimes we fall off them.

Sometimes the best ministry we can offer is simply proving that survival is possible. That you can lose what you can't live without and somehow keep living. That faith can survive even when it feels like God has abandoned you.

The Workshop of Suffering

There's this passage in Hebrews that used to make me angry: "No discipline seems pleasant at the time, but painful. Later on, however, it produces a harvest of righteousness and peace for those who have been trained by it" (Hebrews 12:11, NIV).

I actually threw my Bible once after reading that verse. Hit the wall in my Hong Kong apartment, leaving a dent. My neighbor, Mrs. Chen, banged on the wall and yelled something in Cantonese that probably wasn't "Praise the Lord." I yelled back, "Sorry," and then sat there looking at the dent, wondering if that was also somehow producing a harvest of righteousness.

Trained by it. Like suffering is some kind of spiritual CrossFit gym where God is the trainer yelling "One more rep!" while you're already collapsed on the floor. But I've come to understand it differently.

Training implies intention. Purpose. Progression. It implies that the pain isn't random, isn't meaningless, and isn't God amusing Himself with our struggles. It's preparation for something we can't see yet.

I think about my high school football coach, Coach Williams, five-foot-six of compressed rage and disappointment. Made us run suicides in August, Texas heat until kids puked. We hated him. Called him names I can't write in a Christian book. But senior year, when we made it to the state semifinals and were still standing in the fourth quarter while the other team was gasping, we understood. The pain had a purpose we couldn't see while we were experiencing it.

Not saying God is like Coach Williams, God doesn't wear polyester shorts or smell like Ben-Gay and broken dreams. But maybe the principle is the same. The pain that feels pointless might be preparing us for something we can't imagine yet.

I think about Olympic athletes. The hours in the gym when nobody's watching. The injuries that don't make the highlight reel. The sacrifices that never get mentioned in the gold medal ceremony. Nobody sees the 4 AM training sessions, the ice baths, the physical therapy, the times they wanted to quit but didn't.

When Calling Emerges from Crisis

Here's something I've noticed: most people discover their calling not in moments of clarity but in moments of crisis. Moses found his calling in the desert while running from a murder charge. Paul found his calling blind on a road, having just been knocked off his high horse (literally). Peter discovered his calling after denying Jesus three times and thinking his ministry was over before it began.

My calling emerged from that Caribbean road. Not immediately, took me seventeen years, actually. Seventeen years of running, drinking, marrying the wrong people, building businesses to avoid building character. Seventeen years of telling myself I was fine while falling apart in increasingly creative ways.

The moment it clicked was anticlimactic. Tuesday morning, October 8, 2011. I was sitting in a Starbucks in Kowloon, the one near the harbor where tourists take pictures, drinking a venti Pike Place that tasted like burnt rubber. Reading my Bible app because it was the only thing I actually kept with me in those days. When you're living out of suitcases and sprinting across time zones, a physical Bible becomes one more thing to forget. But the app? That was always in my pocket, even when the rest of my life felt scattered.

Luke 22:32 popped up in the verse of the day: "But I have prayed for you, Simon, that your faith may not fail. And when you have turned back, strengthen your brothers" (NIV).

Simon. My name. Jesus was talking to Peter, but might as well have been talking to me. "When you have turned back," not if, when, "strengthen your brothers."

My calling emerged from that Caribbean road. Not immediately, it took years of running, denying, bargaining, and finally accepting. But eventually, I realized that my accident, my failures, my struggles with faith weren't disqualifications from ministry. They were my qualifications.

Who better to sit with someone processing guilt than someone who's been crushed by it? Who better to talk about starting over than someone who's done it three times? Who better to speak about God's grace than someone who doesn't deserve it but received it anyway?

I started small. Started with just showing up to that Tuesday morning men's group in Hong Kong, the one that met at 6 AM in a community center that smelled like old soy sauce and industrial floor cleaner. Seven guys, all expats, all carrying something heavy.

First time I shared my story, really shared it, not the sanitized version, my hands shook so bad I had to sit on them. Voice cracked when I got to the part about the sound, that specific sound of impact that lives in your bones. One guy, an Australian named Pete, who worked in shipping, just nodded and said, "Mate, that's proper heavy. Thanks for trusting us with it."

That's when I learned: your mess becomes your message, but only after it's been through the refiner's fire.

The Refiner's Fire (It's Hotter Than You Think)

Malachi talks about God being like a refiner's fire, purifying silver and gold (Malachi 3:2-3). I used to think that was a nice metaphor until I actually watched a silversmith at work during a trip to Taxco, Mexico, the silver capital of the world.

December 2017, a work trip that turned into something else. Taxco is built on the side of a mountain, all cobblestone streets and white buildings with red tile roofs, like someone stacked a wedding cake on a hill and forgot to level it. Every other shop sells silver. The sound of hammering on metal is the city's heartbeat.

The silversmith's shop was down an alley that smelled like metal and charcoal, tucked between a taco stand and a shop selling religious icons. Juan Carlos, third-generation silversmith, had scarred hands like a map of every piece he'd ever made.

The silversmith, an old man whose hands told stories of decades at his craft, explained the process. "Silver melts at 961.8 degrees Celsius," he said in accented English. "But the impurities, they burn off at different temperatures. Some lower, some higher. So, I have to keep the silver in the fire, watching."

He had this ancient crucible, which looked like it belonged in a museum. The silver inside was molten, angry, bubbling as if it were fighting the process. The heat coming off it made my eyes water from six feet away.

"Most people want to rush," he said, adjusting the flame with the precision of a heart surgeon. "They see the silver melt, they think it's ready. But melted is not pure. Pure takes time. Pure takes patience. Pure takes heat that seems like destruction."

"How do you know when it's pure?" I asked.

He smiled, the kind of smile that comes from answering this question a thousand times. "When I can see my reflection in it."

He pulled out a piece he'd finished that morning, a small cross, simple, no ornamentation. Held it up to the light. On its surface, distorted but clear, I could see his face reflected. Sixty years of working with fire, and he still got excited about that moment.

"Every time," he said, "every time I see my face in the silver, I think of God seeing His face in us. But first, "he gestured to the crucible, "first comes the fire."

I stood there, watching the silver bubble and transform in the crucible, and thought about all the times I'd felt like I was melting, burning, being destroyed. Maybe I wasn't being destroyed. Maybe I was being refined. Maybe God was burning off everything that wasn't essential, everything that wasn't eternal, everything that kept His image from being clearly reflected in me.

Practical Ways to Process Your Pain

After years of wrestling with this stuff, plus therapy with Dr. Evelyn Hart—who has this gift of calling out my BS while still making me feel loved—here's what actually helps.

Years later, even her once-perfect office had softened. I can still picture that space on Westheimer, the beige walls she swore were "therapeutic," and that same leather chair, worn now from years of tears and truth-telling, that probably knows more secrets than the CIA.

Our breakthrough session was on May 14, 2019. I'd been seeing her for six months, still dancing around the real stuff. She looked at me over those reading glasses she wears on a chain like someone's grandmother and said, "Simon, we can keep talking about your business stress, or we can talk about the man who died. Your choice, but you're paying either way."

Write it out uncensored: Keep a journal where you can be completely honest with God. No religious language required. No "thee" and "thou" nonsense. Just raw, unfiltered truth. Some nights mine are prayers. Some nights they're accusations. Some nights it's just "Why?" written over and over until my hand cramps.

My journal is a black Moleskine I bought at Target while it was on clearance. $7.99, marked down from $24.99, which felt like a metaphor for my life, dramatically reduced. Some entries are illegible because I was crying while writing. Some are in all caps because I was screaming on paper. One entire page is just the F-word written 147 times (I counted later, when I was sane).

Find your fellow sufferers: After my second divorce, I tried to go it alone. Big mistake. Huge. We need people who will sit with us in the mess without trying to fix it, explain it, or spiritualize it. I found mine at a Tuesday morning men's group. We meet at 6 AM, an ungodly hour, but these guys have seen me at my worst and keep showing up.

We call ourselves the "Dead Men Walking" because we all should be dead, from addiction, suicide attempts, accidents, and cancer. But we're not. We're inexplicably alive and trying to figure out what to do with these bonus years.

Jim brings donuts from Shipley's, the kind with enough sugar to make you see God or have a heart attack, maybe both. We meet in this old Sunday school room off the side hallway of the church, the one with the humming fluorescent lights and the AC that only works when it feels like it. We sit in a circle of mismatched chairs and tell the truth. No fixing, no advice unless someone asks, just truth and presence and awful coffee that Mike brews way too strong because he's still calibrated to prison coffee standards.

Serve through your suffering: This sounds backwards, but it works. When I was drowning in guilt after the accident, my pastor suggested volunteering with our church's grief support ministry. "But I don't have answers," I protested. "Good," he said. "People in grief don't need answers. They need presence."

At the first grief support meeting I attended, I sat in the parking lot for twenty minutes, engine running, AC blasting, trying to talk myself into going in. Finally went in because I'd already driven there, and gas is expensive.

The group leader, a widow named Dorothy who'd lost her husband to ALS, opened with: "We're all here because love hurts and death is stupid." No Bible verse, no platitude, just truth. I knew I was in the right place.

Give yourself permission to not be okay: Christians are terrible at this. We think we need to slap on a smile and quote Philippians 4:13, but Jesus wept. Jesus asked for the cup to pass. Jesus cried out, "My God, why have you forsaken me?" If the Son of God can express pain, so can you.

The Long View of Suffering

Here's what I wish someone had told me earlier: suffering isn't a sprint. It's a marathon where someone keeps moving the finish line. Some pain you'll carry your whole life. It changes, softens maybe, but doesn't disappear. And that's okay.

I still think about that night in the Caribbean. Every. Single. Day. Not every minute anymore, used to be every minute, then every hour. Now it's maybe three or four times a day. Progress, Dr. Chen calls it. I call it learning to carry weight without dropping it.

The reminders come at odd times. Driving at dusk when the light looks like that night. Seeing someone in dark clothes crossing against the light. The specific sound of brakes that couldn't stop in time, I heard it last week when someone almost hit a dog, and I had to pull over because I couldn't breathe.

I still think about him—the man whose name I'll never forget. I don't know what his life was like beyond that moment, but I imagine it was full of work, family, and small joys that filled ordinary days. The irony is not lost on me that he trusted God's timing, and I've spent years wrestling with it.

The weight has changed; it's no longer crushing, but it's still there. Like a stone in my pocket that I feel whenever I reach for my keys. A reminder of fragility, of consequences, of grace.

Some people get healing. Some get miracles. Some of us get just enough grace for today, with the promise of more tomorrow. And maybe that's its own kind of miracle.

Your Deeper Why

If you're reading this from your own pit right now, let me tell you something: your story isn't over. I know it feels like it. I know some days you can barely remember who you were before the pain. But God specializes in plot twists.

I'm writing this at 5:23 AM on January 15, 2022, in my garage office in Texas. Kids are still asleep. Stefaniya is probably awake but pretending to sleep so she doesn't have to deal with morning chaos yet. Coffee's getting cold. Back hurts from this cheap office chair I refuse to replace because suffering builds character or something.

Ten years ago, I was divorced, drunk, and convinced God was done with me. Today, I'm married to a woman who sees my scars as stories, not shame. I have three kids who think I'm a hero even though I've told them I'm not. I have a ministry born from mess, where I get to sit with broken people and say, "Me too. But watch what God does with broken things."

My accident led me to understand grace in ways success never could have. My divorces taught me about commitment in ways that an easy marriage never would have. My business failures showed me that my worth isn't tied to my net worth. My journey through different denominations taught me that God is bigger than our boxes.

Specific revelations from specific pain:

• The accident taught me that forgiveness is a daily choice, not a one-time feeling

- First divorce taught me that you can't fix someone who doesn't want to be fixed

- Second divorce taught me that running to a new geography doesn't fix old problems

- Business failure taught me that God's economy runs on different metrics than Wall Street

- Depression taught me that sometimes the bravest thing is just staying alive

- My kids' questions taught me that faith isn't about having answers but being honest about the questions

Your suffering has a purpose. Not because God needs your pain, He doesn't. But because He refuses to waste it. Every tear is collected. Every prayer is heard. Every broken piece is being fitted into a mosaic you can't see yet.

YOUR NEXT STEP

This week, write a letter to God about your suffering. Not a prayer, a letter. Tell Him exactly how you feel about what you've been through. Don't clean it up. Don't make it sound spiritual. Just be honest.

Here's the beginning of mine from last week:

"Dear God, I'm still pissed about the Caribbean. I know it's been 28 years, but some angers age like wine, they get more complex with time. I'm angry you didn't stop it. I'm angry you let me live with it. I'm angry that grace doesn't erase consequences.

But I'm also grateful. (This feels like betrayal to write.) Grateful that my worst moment became my watershed moment. Grateful that

You've used my guilt to help others process theirs. Grateful that his death wasn't wasted, even though I wish it never happened.

I don't understand You. Most days I'm not sure I even like You. But I can't seem to quit You. Which is either faith or Stockholm syndrome.

Still here, still angry, still Yours (somehow), Simon"

Then identify one person who needs to hear your survival story. Not your victory story, your survival story. The messy middle where you're still figuring it out, but you're still standing. Share it with them.

Last week, I shared with Trevor, the kid who lost his baby. Took him to that Thai place where the pad-thai is terrible but the privacy is good—told him about our miscarriages, all three of them, before Alex was born. Told him about sitting in a CVS parking lot, crying because Stefaniya had sent me to buy pads, the industrial kind for after a miscarriage, and I couldn't find the right ones, and somehow that felt like failing her again.

He said, "So it doesn't get easier?"

"No," I said. "It gets different. You learn to carry it. And eventually, impossibly, you'll help someone else carry theirs."

Because here's what I've learned: we don't need more success stories in the church. We need more survival stories. Stories that say, "I'm still here. Still breathing. Still believing, even when belief feels impossible."

Your worst moment might be the very thing that qualifies you to speak hope into someone else's darkness. Your deepest wound might become the well from which others drink living water.

That's not consolation prize theology. That's the economy of the Kingdom, where the last are first, the weak are strong, and the broken become beautiful.

Even you. Especially and always you.

Alex just walked into my office, the one with skinned knees from the beginning of this chapter. Band-aids starting to peel off, scabs forming underneath. "Daddy, does God ever explain why bad things happen?"

"Not usually, buddy. But He shows up in them."

"Like you showed up when I fell?"

"Yeah, exactly like that."

He thought about it, then said, "I still don't like falling."

"Me neither, son. Me neither."

But we're still riding. Still falling. Still getting back up. Still believing that somehow, in ways we can't see yet, the falling is teaching us to fly.

That's faith. That's the deeper why. That's God's plan working through your breakthrough.

EPILOGUE

Moving Forward

I'm sitting here in my home office, the same one where this whole journey on MS Word began. Looking at that photo from Hong Kong where I met Stefaniya, both of us looking younger, less tired, unaware of the kids and chaos and beauty that would follow. Next to it sits my beat-up Bible from 2000, held together with duct tape and prayer, pages falling out like autumn leaves. Funny how life works out differently from how we plan.

The photo is from March 14, 2015, that church potluck where Stefaniya wore the sunflower dress. Someone took it with my phone, probably Viktor, his thumbs in the corner. We're both holding paper plates with food we couldn't identify, smiling like idiots who don't know they're about to change each other's lives. The Bible is NIV, bought at LifeWay Christian Store in Houston for $39.99, back when I thought expensive Bibles made you holier. Genesis is missing pages 1-47. Revelation ends at chapter 20. The duct tape is silver, the Home Depot brand, applied during a particularly aggressive wrestling match with Romans 8.

It's November 22, 2024, 6:14 AM. Thanksgiving in two days. The cursor blinks at me, waiting for some profound conclusion to this mess of a testimony. Outside, our neighbor's rooster, yes, we have a neighbor with a rooster in suburban Texas, is announcing dawn like he invented it.

Can I tell you a secret about breakthroughs? They rarely feel like breakthroughs when you're in the middle of them. They usually come disguised as breakdowns. At least mine did.

The Truth Nobody Wants to Hear

When I was ten years old, drafting house plans with that wine cellar I thought meant success, I had no idea those plans would take me through hell before finding any heaven. That kid with brown eyes and too much ambition couldn't imagine he'd end up walking the streets of Ephesus, where Paul preached, trying to understand how God could use someone who'd taken a life. When I was crying on the top bunk listening to my parents fight downstairs, I couldn't imagine I'd one day be teaching my own kids about resilient faith, about how sometimes love means staying when everything in you wants to run.

Found those house plans last month while cleaning out the garage. Yellowed notebook paper, Big Chief tablet, the kind with the Native American chief on the cover that probably wouldn't fly today. My ten-year-old handwriting, all capitals because I thought architects wrote in capitals. The wine cellar was labeled "DADDY'S SPECIAL ROOM" with a note: "NO KIDS ALLOWED." Even drew little wine bottles on shelves. Kid had no idea his daddy's special room would become a garage in Texas where he'd cry and pray and write a book about failing forward.

Here's what I've learned after all these years, all these miles, all these mistakes: God's plan rarely looks like our plan. Thank God for that. Because my plan would have protected me from the very things that shaped me into someone who could actually help others.

What Real Resilience Looks Like

Let me tell you what resilience actually looks like, because it's not what you see on motivational posters with sunrise backgrounds and cursive fonts.

Resilience is getting baptized in 2000, thinking you've got it all figured out with your new LDS faith, then watching your marriage fall apart even though you're doing everything by the book. It's leaving a church you love because staying would mean living a lie.

That baptism: January 15, 2000, 3 PM, Copperfield Ward, Houston Texas North Stake. Water temperature exactly 98.6°F because they have a thermometer and everything. Bishop Anderson dunked me, had to do it twice because my foot popped up the first time, apparently even my body parts resist submission. Elizabeth cried. I thought they were happy tears. Looking back, maybe she already knew what I couldn't see, that perfect religion can't fix imperfect people.

Resilience is moving to Hong Kong for business, thinking you're running away from failure, only to meet the woman God had planned for you all along at a Slavic community gathering where you understood nothing except that you belonged. (Natalya, if you ever read this, спасибо. That one introduction changed everything.)

Resilience is writing this book with hands that still shake when I remember that night in the Caribbean, but writing it anyway because someone needs to know that God uses broken people, not despite their brokenness, but because of it.

Building Your Own Breakthrough

After all this living, here's my framework for finding a breakthrough in breakdown. Call it the "Three-Day Rule of Surrender" because it usually takes me about three days to stop fighting God and actually surrender whatever I'm white-knuckling.

Discovered this pattern in 2020 when Stefaniya was pregnant with Evan, and the doctor said there might be complications. Spent three days in the following predictable cycle:

Monday, 2:30 PM: "This isn't happening. The doctor's wrong. We'll get a second opinion. I'll research everything. I'll fix this." Tuesday, 10:45 AM: "Okay God, if You heal this, I'll go to church every Sunday, twice on Easter. I'll tithe 15%. I'll stop cussing in traffic." Wednesday, 6:22 PM: "I can't. I literally cannot do this. It's Yours. Take it. Please."

Evan was born perfect. Well, perfect except for his ability to scream at frequencies that should be illegal.

Day one: Denial. "This isn't happening. I can fix this. I don't need help." Day two: Bargaining. "Okay God, if You fix this, I'll do whatever You want." Day three: Surrender. "I can't do this. It's Yours. Help."

I learned this pattern through repetition. Lost count of how many three-day cycles I've been through. But here's what I've discovered: God is patient enough to wait for day three. Every time.

The Question That Changes Everything

Here's the question I've learned to ask in every situation: "God, what are You trying to teach me here?"

Not "Why is this happening?" That's usually unanswerable this side of heaven. Not "When will this end?" God's timeline never matches ours. But "What are You teaching me?" that's always answerable if we're willing to listen.

Started keeping a "Lessons Journal" in 2019. Just a composition notebook from Walmart, $0.97. Sample entries:

Lesson from losing the Peterson contract: "My security isn't in contracts but in Christ. Also, maybe don't put all eggs in one client basket."

Lesson from Alex's seizure at six months: "I'm not in control. Never was. Thank God for that because I would've screwed it up."

Lesson from the transmission dying in my truck at 267,000 miles: "All things die. It's okay. Also, maybe maintain vehicles better."

Because He's always teaching something. Always shaping. Always working that plan we can't see.

When my business failed, He was teaching me that my worth isn't in my net worth. When my marriages ended, He was teaching me that you can't build lasting love on a foundation of unprocessed pain. When I met Stefaniya, He was teaching me that redemption often comes from unexpected places, with unexpected accents, at unexpected times.

The Truth About That Night

You know what nobody tells you about breakthroughs? They usually cost everything you thought you couldn't live without. That night on a Caribbean island, when someone's life ended and mine continued, I felt God had made a terrible mistake. Why take him and leave me? Thirty years later, I think I understand, not the why (I'll never understand the why this side of heaven) but the what now.

I often think about the man whose life ended that night. I don't know his story, not really. I don't know his age, his family, his work, or what he loved. All I know is that he was a human being with a life in motion, a life that should have continued. And I think about how none of us ever imagine that an ordinary day could be our last. We assume we have more time. Most of us do—until one moment says otherwise.

I read the official report years later. There were no dramatic details, no final conversations captured on record, just the quiet outline of a life interrupted. Somehow, that silence stayed with me more than anything else. The reminder that a typical morning can carry a night we never see coming.

Maybe that's what faith really is—the courage to live in that space between what we expect and what we cannot control.

What I do know is this: a life ended, and mine kept going. That reality has shaped every hard conversation I've had since. Every person I've sat with in their guilt. Every marriage I've fought for because I couldn't save my first two. Every moment, I've whispered "Grace is still real" to someone who can't believe it. That's the "what now."

And whoever that family is—however many of them there were—they've stayed in my prayers every day. I ask God to bring beauty from their ashes, too. I may never know what redemption looks like on their side of the story, but I trust it came. God has a way of working in places our eyes will never see.

Your Story Is Still Being Written

If you're reading this from your own pit right now, maybe it's divorce papers on your kitchen counter, maybe it's a diagnosis you didn't see coming, maybe it's guilt you've carried so long it feels like part of your DNA, let me tell you something: your story isn't over.

I'm writing this final section while Alex practices piano in the living room. He's murdering "Jingle Bells" with the enthusiasm of someone who thinks volume equals talent. Evan's arguing with Stefaniya about why he can't wear his Halloween costume to Thanksgiving. Olivia just drew on the wall with a marker, again. This is my life now. Chaos and beauty and marker on walls I'll have to repaint.

Ten years ago, I was drunk in a Hong Kong 7-Eleven bathroom at 3 AM, convinced my story was over. Today I'm a father, husband, author (apparently), and someone who gets to tell others that rock bottom is just a foundation.

I know it feels final. I know some days you can barely remember who you were before the pain. But God specializes in plot twists. He's the author who brings dead characters back to life, who turns villains into heroes, who makes beauty from ashes.

Final Thoughts from a Fellow Traveler

I'm not writing this as someone who's arrived. Yesterday I lost my temper in traffic. Last week I skipped church to watch football. This morning, I had to apologize to Stefaniya for something I said when I was hangry. I'm writing as someone still traveling, still learning that faith is less about answers and more about trust. Still occasionally crying out, "I believe; help my unbelief!" (Mark 9:24, NIV).

But I'm also writing as someone who's seen God show up in the strangest places. In a Russian church in Hong Kong, where I understood nothing but felt everything. In a Miami men's group meeting in a moldy portable building. In a hospital room where our third child almost didn't make it but did, Olivia, our miracle baby, currently eating goldfish crackers off the floor because third kids raise themselves.

Your breakthrough might be closer than you think. Or it might look completely different from what you expect. Either way, God's got this. And He's got you.

Keep walking. Keep trusting. Keep your eyes open for grace in unexpected places; it usually shows up looking nothing like you'd expect, speaking languages you don't understand, offering hope when you've forgotten what hope looks like.

And remember, we're all just walking each other home. Every broken one of us. Every failure. Every success that felt like failure. Every prayer felt unheard. We're all just stumbling toward grace together.

As I write this last paragraph, Stefaniya just brought me coffee, real coffee, not the instant stuff, because "life's too short for bad coffee" even eleven years into marriage. The mug says "World's Okayest Dad" (Alex picked it out). She kisses my forehead, says something in Ukrainian I still don't understand but know means love, and reminds me that Thanksgiving prep starts in two hours.

This is my breakthrough: A woman who loves me despite everything. Kids who think I'm a hero even though I've told them the truth. A garage office where I write about pain and grace. Coffee that's still hot. A God who still shows up.

Your breakdown? It's not the end of your story. It's the chapter where everything changes. Where you discover strength you didn't know existed. Where grace shows up in work clothes, ready to rebuild.

Trust the process. Trust the pain. Trust the God who specializes in resurrection.

Your breakthrough is coming. It might not look like you imagined. Mine certainly didn't. But it's coming.

Hold on.

"Every scar has a story. Every story needs a witness. Every witness becomes a bridge." — Simon Rockwell, November 2025

DISCUSSION GUIDE

From Breakdown to Breakthrough

God's Plan, Your Breakthrough: From Breakdown to Breakthrough

How to Use This Guide: This isn't a test. It's a tool for transformation. Work through it with brutal honesty, whether alone with a journal or in a group willing to drop masks. Keep tissues handy. And coffee. Definitely coffee.

1. **Materials needed:** Index cards, journal, ugly chair, duct tape (seriously)

2. **Gordon Check:** Look for your own "Gordon the Gecko" - that weird constant in your chaos

Chapter 1: Faith in Motion

Deeper Dive Questions:

1. **The 4:47 AM Principle:** Simon meets God when insomnia strikes. *What's your "worst time" that could become your holy time?* Set your alarm for that time tomorrow. Just once. See what happens.

2. **The Parking Lot Moment:** Simon had his prostate scare revelation in a Whataburger parking lot. Draw a map of where you've actually met God (not where you think you should have). Mark the weird places with stars.

3. **Action Challenge:** This week, pray somewhere ridiculous. A

241

drive-through. A bathroom stall. The DMV. Document what changes when you stop waiting for the "right" setting.

4. **The Three Clicks:** What's your 'three clicks' warning sign that reality is about to hit? Dr. Ramirez clicked his pen three times before delivering bad news. What's your warning signal?

Group Exercise: Everyone shares their most ungodly prayer location. No judgment. Prize for weirdest spot.

Chapter 2: Stories That Strengthen

Transformation Questions:

1. **The Martinez Method:** Brother Martinez wore his tear tattoos without explanation. What visible scar do you hide that could become someone's hope?

2. **Testimony Audit:** Write two versions of your testimony:

    i. Version A: The cleaned-up Sunday version

    ii. Version B: The Friday-night-breakdown version

Which one would actually help someone at rock bottom?

3. **The Receipt Challenge:** Martinez gave his number on a Home Depot receipt. This week, give your number to someone who looks like they're barely holding on. Use whatever paper you have.

4. **The Dorothy Detail:** "Who's your dollar-store-card person who won't give up on you?"

Accountability Exercise: Text your group one raw truth about your story you've never shared in church.

Chapter 3: Pain with Purpose

Wrestling Questions:

1. **Museum Curator:** Design three plaques for your "Museum of Mistakes." Include:

    i.   The mistake

    ii. The current damage assessment

    iii. The redemption potential (even if you can't see it yet)

2. **The Irreversible:** Simon can't undo the Caribbean accident. What's your un-undoable? Write a letter to it, not asking for erasure but for purpose.

3. **Rock Bottom Geography:** Map your various rock bottoms (financial, spiritual, relational, physical). Which one are you still at? Circle it. That's where God's working hardest.

4. **The Rock-Bottom Number:** Write your exact rock-bottom number. Simon had $247 in his checking account. Frame it when you recover.

Practical Application: Create an actual "Ebenezer stone" this week. A physical reminder. Not pretty. Just real.

Chapter 4: Sacred Reflection

Prayer Revolution:

1. **The Screenshot Prayer Test:** Simon's group prayed about their most-used apps. Do it. Right now. What does your digital footprint say about your spiritual priorities?

2. **Three-Word Honesty:** Simon started with "Still here, God."

Write your three words on your bathroom mirror. Update them weekly.

3. **Sacred Space Audit:** Where's your duct-tape-and-prayer corner? If you don't have one, claim one this week. Ugly is fine. Ugly might be better.

4. **Napkin Prayer:** "Reference Simon's Hong Kong prayer napkin specifically. Write your rawest prayer on a napkin. Keep it until answered (or forever if that's what it takes).

Weekly Practice: Send one voice-text prayer to God daily. Yes, actually record it. Yes, it'll feel weird. Do it anyway.

Chapter 5: Faith Together

Community Challenge:

1. **The Mike Test:** Who would knock on your truck window if they saw divorce papers? If nobody comes to mind, that's your real problem. Fix it.

2. **Mismatched Chairs Ministry:** The best community happens in broken places. Where's your portable building with mildew? Find it or create it.

3. **The Eduardo Effect:** This week, make one introduction that could change someone's life. Don't overthink it. Just connect two people who need each other.

4. **The Borscht Moment:** "When did you meet grace covered in mess (literal or figurative)? Simon met Stefaniya while wearing beet soup. What was your 'borscht spill' that revealed real love?"

Group Covenant: Everyone commits to one "me too" moment in this meeting. No advice allowed. Just witness.

Chapter 6: Anchored in the Word

Scripture Saturation:

1. **The Index Card Invasion:** Pick one verse. Write it on seven index cards. Put them:

    i. In your shoe (you'll feel it all day)

    ii. On your steering wheel

    iii. In your wallet

    iv. On your coffee maker

    v. Wherever you hide your vice

    vi. On your pillow

    vii. In your pocket

2. **SCRIPT Method Practice:** Take your current crisis and run it through:

    i. Scripture: What verse fights this?

    ii. Context: What was happening when it was written?

    iii. Reflection: How does it hit your specific situation?

    iv. Insight: What's God saying you don't want to hear?

    v. Practical: What changes today?

    vi. Testimony: Who needs to hear what you learned?

3. **The Mockingbird Sermon:** "What everyday annoyance might be God's repetitive lesson? That bird outside Simon's window wouldn't shut up until he listened. What won't stop repeating in your life?"

Accountability: Text your verse to someone every morning at 4:47 AM for a week. Yes, that early. That's the point.

Chapter 7: Divine Perspective

Reframe Exercises:

1. **Kintsugi Project:** Break something on purpose. Fix it badly, but obviously. Display it prominently. Tell everyone who asks why it's beautiful.

2. **The Silversmith Test:** What's God burning out of you right now? Name it. Thank Him for the fire (through gritted teeth is fine).

3. **Credentialed by Crisis:** List three ways your worst failure qualified you to help someone. Contact one of those someone's this week.

4. **Recognition Moment:** Who can see you've been 'broken and rebuilt'? Patricia from Trinidad saw it in Simon immediately. Ask them what they see.

Visual Reminder: Take a photo of something broken but still functioning in your house. Make it your phone wallpaper.

Chapter 8: One Church, Many Stories

Global Faith Challenge:

1. **Finger Scripture:** Like Chen's grandmother, memorize one verse using only your fingers as a reminder. No paper. Just flesh and memory.

2. **Coffee or Poison:** Yusuf chose coffee. What's your daily choice between bitterness and blessing? Set an alarm for that decision time.

3. **Language Barrier Love:** This month, serve somewhere where you don't speak the language. Find God in the confusion.

4. **Language of Faith:** Find a faith community that doesn't speak your language. Stay anyway. Watch how love translates.

Cultural Expansion: Learn to pray the Lord's Prayer in another language. Pray it daily until it feels natural.

Chapter 9: Gratitude as a Weapon

Gratitude Warfare:

1. **The Morning Three:** For 30 days, no exceptions:

    i. Write three things on index cards every morning

    ii. Include one that's absurdly small (like Gordon the gecko)

    iii. Include one that hurts to be grateful for

    iv. Include one that makes you laugh

2. **Crisis Gratitude:** Write five things you're grateful for about your worst current situation. If you can't find five, find one. Start there.

3. **Gratitude Contamination:** Leave your gratitude cards where others will find them. Spread the infection.

4. **Running Toward Breakthrough:** What breakthrough came from running away? Simon fled on Flight SQ890. Thank God for the flight that led you home.

Extreme Challenge: Thank God for something that destroyed you. Out loud. Mean it (even 1% counts).

Chapter 10: God's Deeper Why

Purpose in Pain:

1. **Question Flip:** Replace every "Why, God?" with "What are You teaching me?" for one week. Document the difference.

2. **Invisible Training:** List three skills your current suffering is developing. Who will need those exact skills from you later?

3. **The $200 Truth:** What truth do you already know but need someone else to say? Pay someone (therapist, counselor, pastor) to say it. It's worth it.

4. **Failed Formulas:** List three 'Christian formulas' that failed you. Trevor lost his baby despite doing everything "right." Find the grace in formula failure.

Legacy Letter: Write to someone who will face your current trial in ten years. Tell them what you wish you'd known.

Epilogue: Moving Forward

Breakthrough Blueprint:

1. **Three-Day Surrender Cycle:** Where are you today?

    i. Day 1: Denial (This isn't happening)

    ii. Day 2: Bargaining (God, if You fix this...)

    iii. Day 3: Surrender (Okay, use this mess) Mark it on your calendar. Track your patterns.

2. **Childhood Dreams Redemption:** Find something you wanted at age 10. How is God giving it to you differently now?

3. **Forever Prayers:** Who are you praying for that you'll never see

results for? Commit to praying anyway. Daily. Until you die.

4.   **Holy Interruptions:** How do frozen waffle requests interrupt your theology? Why is that perfect? What mundane need keeps pulling you back to earth?

Final Assignment: Write your own "breakdown to breakthrough" story in exactly 500 words. Share it with someone in breakdown. This week.

21-Day Transformation Challenge

1.   **Week 1: Honesty**

    i.   Days 1-7: Tell the ugly truth (to God, yourself, one other person)

2.   **Week 2: Community**

    i.   Days 8-14: Show up messy (no cleanup allowed)

3.   **Week 3: Gratitude**

    i.   Days 15-21: Thank God for the disaster (even through gritted teeth)

4.   **Group Covenant**

    i.   If using this guide together, commit to:

        a.   **No fixing** (witness, don't solve)

        b.   **No faking** (bring your real self)

        c.   **No fleeing** (stay when it gets uncomfortable)

Final Reflection

Your breakdown isn't the end of your story. It's the chapter where everything changes. This guide isn't about feeling better. It's about becoming who you're meant to be through the breaking.

As Simon says, "We're all just walking each other home."

So, walk. Limp if you have to. But walk together.

The only wrong answer is pretending you have it all together.

Now stop reading guides and start living the breakthrough.

Even if you're still in the breakdown.

Especially then.

Simon's Benediction

If this guide doesn't make you uncomfortable, you're not doing it right.

If it doesn't make you cry at least once, keep digging.

If it doesn't make you wrestle with God before resting in Him, you're still performing.

Stop performing.

Start opening.

Break open the things inside you that were never meant to stay sealed — the pride, the shame, the stories you've tried to outrun.

That's where breakthrough begins.

And remember: Gordon the Gecko is watching. So is God.

Gordon judges your coffee choices. God doesn't.

Focus on the right witness.

You don't need to break anything physical.

Just loosen your grip on whatever you've been white-knuckling.

Let something internal surrender... and trust God to rebuild what actually matters.

Even if you can't see how yet.

Especially then.

Copyright Note: *This Discussion Guide is part of "God's Plan, Your Breakthrough" by Simon Rockwell, published by JLS Publishers, LLC. Permission granted to reproduce for small group use only.*

GOD'S PLAN SMALL GROUP TOOLKIT

For Group Facilitators and Members

Small groups work best when the room feels honest and safe. Use this toolkit as a guide to help you lead with humility, wisdom, and grace.

SECTION ONE: Small Group Leader Notes

When Someone Breaks Down

- Do not rush to fix anything
- Do not preach a verse at them
- Sit with them
- Pass tissues
- Share your own moment of breaking if it fits

Presence often heals more than speeches.

When Discussion Stalls

- Begin with your own fresh failure
- Ask: What happened this week that you have not said out loud yet
- Lead a symbolic release: a paper you tear, a stone you drop, a burden you name

(Do not break physical objects. Safety first.)

Silence is not an enemy.

It is often the doorway to truth.

When the Room Feels Heavy

- Remind them Gordon the Gecko survived worse
- Humor is welcome
- God meets people in parking lots, kitchens, and late-night grocery aisles
- Take a coffee break when needed

A heavy room is often a holy room.

Keep On Hand

- Crisis hotline numbers
- Local counselor and pastoral care referrals
- Extra index cards
- Tissues
- Coffee
- One intentionally ugly chair for the prayer corner

Important Note for Facilitators

Group leaders offer support, not therapy.

You are not responsible for fixing anyone.

If someone shares thoughts of self-harm, unsafe situations, domestic violence, or dangerous substance use, pause the group and guide them toward professional help.

Use the crisis resources provided.

SECTION TWO: Trauma-Informed Guidance

Some people will share things they have never said aloud.

Your response matters.

What To Do

- Stay calm
- Listen without interrupting
- Keep your voice gentle and slow
- Acknowledge their courage
- Pause the room if emotions overwhelm
- Offer grounding statements such as: You are safe here or Thank you for trusting us

Your steadiness becomes their anchor.

What Not To Do

- Do not probe for details
- Do not interpret their story
- Do not offer spiritual clichés
- Do not promise outcomes you cannot guarantee

Pain deserves respect, not shortcuts.

When Someone Is in Crisis

Stop the group immediately if someone expresses:

- Thoughts of self-harm
- Intent to hurt others
- Abuse or unsafe home situations
- Severe substance dependency
- Emotional overwhelm they cannot regulate

Stay with them.

Use the crisis resource list.

Guide them toward professional help.

Your Role

Hold space with compassion.

Let professionals handle the rest.

Trust God with what you cannot carry.

SECTION THREE: Small Group Covenant

Read this together at the first gathering.

This is how we will show up for one another.

Our Commitment

1. Confidentiality is essential. What is shared here stays here unless someone is in danger.
2. Grace leads us. No judging. No shaming. No correcting motives.
3. We do not fix people. Unsolicited advice blocks real healing.
4. We speak only from our own story. Here is what helped me, not Here is what you should do.
5. We make room for emotion. Tears, silence, and frustration are all welcome.
6. We remove the masks. No pretending. No performance.
7. We honor time. We show up when we can and communicate when we cannot.
8. We trust God with the rebuilding. We open the door. God does the work.
9. Together we say: We will hold this space with grace and courage.

SECTION FOUR: Facilitator Prayer

God our Father and Lord Jesus Christ,

Give me ears that listen more than I speak.

Give me a soft heart for heavy stories.

Give me wisdom to know when to speak and humility to know when to stay quiet.

Let this room become a place where masks fall away and grace rises up.

Guide me without pride.

Protect me from fear.

Let Your Spirit heal what we cannot.

I pray in the name of Jesus Christ, Amen.

SECTION FIVE: Opening and Closing Liturgy

Use this only if it helps your group find rhythm and grounding.

Opening Liturgy

Leader: Tonight, we bring our authentic selves.

Group: Not the polished version. The honest one.

Leader: We bring what is heavy and what is hopeful.

Group: We trust God with both.

Leader: We open our hearts, even the bruised places.

Group: Lord, meet us here.

Closing Liturgy

Leader: We release what we cannot carry.

Group: And we receive the grace we need for today.

Leader: We leave this room held, not alone.

Group: And we trust God with tomorrow.

CRISIS RESOURCES

U.S. & Worldwide

When life hits hard, reach out. You are not meant to carry your pain alone. These resources can help you find steady ground again.

United States Crisis Resources

Immediate Crisis / Mental Health Emergencies

- 988 Suicide & Crisis Lifeline:

- Call or text 988 anytime.

- Free, confidential, available 24/7.

- Crisis Text Line: Text HOME to 741741

- Support via SMS when you can't talk out loud.

- Veterans Crisis Line: Dial 988, then press 1, Text: 838255

- Substance Use & Mental Health (SAMHSA) 1-800-662-HELP (4357). Treatment referrals and information are available 24/7.

Domestic Violence & Safety

- National Domestic Violence Hotline: 1-800-799-SAFE (7233) or text START to 88788

- RAINN – Sexual Assault Hotline 1-800-656-HOPE (4673). Live chat available at www.rainn.org

Finding a Therapist or Counselor

- www.psychologytoday.com
  Search licensed therapists, marriage counselors, and faith-based providers.

- www.faithfulcounseling.com
  Christian therapists offering online and phone sessions.

- www.betterhelp.com
  Online therapy with licensed professionals.

International Crisis Resources (Worldwide)

Global Suicide & Mental Health Directory

- IASP – International Suicide Prevention Directory iasp.info/resources/Crisis_Centres/ (Country-by-country crisis hotlines)

- Befrienders Worldwide: www.befrienders.org (Emotional support centers in 30+ countries)

Europe

- UK & Ireland – Samaritans 116 123 (UK & Ireland)

  o www.samaritans.org

- NHS 111 (UK) For urgent mental health help.

Canada

- Talk Suicide Canada: 1-833-456-4566 or Text 45645

Australia & New Zealand

- Lifeline Australia: 13 11 14

- Lifeline Aotearoa (NZ): 0800 543 354

Asia

- Singapore Samaritans of Singapore (SOS): 1-767

- Hong Kong Samaritans: 2896 0000

Africa

- South Africa Suicide Crisis Line: 0800 567 567

- Lifeline Southern Africa: 0861 322 322

Latin America

- Local hotlines available at www.befrienders.org (Many South American and Caribbean nations listed.)

Substance Use / Addiction Support (Global & Online)

- Alcoholics Anonymous (AA):

  o www.aa.org (meeting finder worldwide)

- Narcotics Anonymous (NA):

  o www.na.org/meetingsearch

- Celebrate Recovery:

  o www.celebraterecovery.com (Christ-centered healing groups)

Faith-Based Support

- Local Church Pastoral Care
  Most churches offer prayer, counseling, and community support.

- Stephen Ministries: www.stephenministries.org (One-on-one Christian caregiving)

- Focus on the Family Counseling Line (US): 1-855-771-HELP (4357)

If You Are in Immediate Danger

Always call your local emergency number (911 in the US, 999 in the UK, 112 in the EU, 000 in Australia). Your safety matters. Please note that contact details may change over time. If a listed resource is unavailable, seek immediate help from local emergency services or a trusted healthcare provider.

A Note from Simon

Asking for help is not weakness.

It is courage.

It is strength.

It is stepping toward the life God still has for you.

You are not alone.

You are not beyond hope.

And you are not too far gone for God to begin again.

Copyright Note: *This Crisis Resource List is part of "God's Plan, Your Breakthrough" by Simon Rockwell, published by JLS Publishers, LLC. Permission granted to reproduce for small group use only.*

REFERENCES

Barna Group. (2020). *Signs of decline & hope among key metrics of faith.* https://www.barna.com/research/changing-state-of-the-church/

Biblica. (2011). *Holy Bible, New International Version.* Biblica. (Original work published 1973)

Bonhoeffer, D. (1954). *Life together* (J. W. Doberstein, Trans.). Harper & Row. (Original work published 1939)

Calhoun, A. A. (2015). *Spiritual disciplines handbook: Practices that transform us* (Rev. ed.). InterVarsity Press.

Cohen, L. (1992). *Anthem* [Song]. On *The Future.* Columbia Records.

Das, R. (2000). *Still here: Embracing aging, changing, and dying.* Riverhead Books.

Emmons, R. A., & McCullough, M. E. (2003). Counting blessings versus burdens: An experimental investigation of gratitude and subjective well-being in daily life. *Journal of Personality and Social Psychology, 84*(2), 377–389. https://doi.org/10.1037/0022-3514.84.2.377

Foster, R. J. (2018). *Celebration of discipline: The path to spiritual growth* (Special anniversary ed.). HarperOne.

Keller, T. (2013). *Walking with God through pain and suffering.* Penguin Books.

Lamott, A. (1999). *Traveling mercies: Some thoughts on faith.* Anchor Books.

Lamott, A. (2012). *Help, thanks, wow: The three essential prayers.* Riverhead Books.

Lewis, C. S. (1961). *A grief observed.* Faber and Faber. (Original work published 1960)

Lewis, C. S. (2001). *The problem of pain.* HarperOne. (Original work published 1940)

Lyubomirsky, S. (2007). *The how of happiness: A scientific approach to getting the life you want.* Penguin Press.

Nouwen, H. J. M. (1994). *The return of the prodigal son: A story of homecoming.* Image Books.

Pew Research Center. (2023). *Modeling the future of religion in America.* https://www.pewresearch.org/religion/2023/09/13/modeling-the-future-of-religion-in-america/

Seligman, M. E. P. (2011). *Flourish: A visionary new understanding of happiness and well-being.* Free Press.

Stanley, A. (2006). *It came from within: The shocking truth of what lurks in the heart.* Multnomah Books.

Tedeschi, R. G., & Calhoun, L. G. (1996). The posttraumatic growth inventory: Measuring the positive legacy of trauma. *Journal of Traumatic Stress, 9*(3), 455–471. https://doi.org/10.1002/jts.2490090305

Tedeschi, R. G., Shakespeare-Finch, J., Taku, K., & Calhoun, L. G. (2018). *Posttraumatic growth: Theory, research, and applications.* Routledge.

Twenge, J. M. (2023). *Generations: The real differences between Gen Z, millennials, Gen X, boomers, and silents.* Atria Books.

Willard, D. (2000). *The divine conspiracy: Rediscovering our hidden life in God* (Reprint ed.). HarperOne.

Wolf, K., & Wolf, J. (2020). *Suffer strong: How to survive anything by redefining everything.* Zondervan.

World Health Organization. (2022). *World mental health report: Transforming mental health for all.* https://www.who.int/publications/i/item/9789240049338

Wright, N. T. (2006). *Evil and the justice of God.* InterVarsity Press.

Wright, N. T. (2014). *Surprised by Scripture: Engaging contemporary issues.* HarperOne.

Yancey, P. (1997). *What's so amazing about grace?* Zondervan.

Zahn, R., Moll, J., Paiva, M. L. M., Garrido, G. E. J., Krueger, F., Huey, E. D., & Grafman, J. (2009). The neural basis of human social values: evidence from functional MRI. *Cerebral Cortex, 19*(2), 276-283.

Additional Note: This book contains personal narratives and experiences. While specific locations, businesses, and some individuals are named, certain names and identifying details have been changed to protect privacy. The author's experiences with various religious denominations and spiritual practices reflect his personal journey and are not intended as theological endorsement or criticism.

Disclaimer: The coping strategies and spiritual practices described in this book represent the author's personal experience and should not replace professional medical or psychological treatment. If you are experiencing mental health challenges, please seek qualified professional help.

THANK YOU FOR READING

Thank you for making it to the end of this book.

I don't take that lightly.

In a world full of noise and endless distractions, choosing to spend your time here means more than I can say. My hope is that these pages encouraged you, challenged you, or helped you see your own story—and God's presence in it—with fresh clarity.

If this book resonated with you, I'd be deeply grateful if you shared a brief review on Amazon or wherever you purchased it. Your honest words not only support this work, but they help others who may be searching for hope, direction, or reassurance that they are not alone.

To leave your feedback:

Open your camera app
Point your phone at the QR code below

Or simply visit: www.jlspublishers.com

Thank you again for walking this part of the journey with me. May God continue to guide, strengthen, and renew you as you move forward. — *Simon Rockwell*

CONTINUE THE JOURNEY

The **Resilience in Faith Series:** *When Everything You Thought Would Save You Doesn't*

The series is just beginning. Each book in this collection offers encouraging stories, biblical wisdom, and practical tools for navigating life's storms with unshakable faith.

Upcoming Books

- **Book 2:** When Church Hurts More Than It Helps
- **Book 3:** Loving Someone Who Sees God Differently
- **Book 4:** Sins of the Father and How You Can Stop Them
- **Book 5:** When Success Becomes Your Secret Addiction

Want free sample chapters, updates, and behind-the-scenes content?

Visit www.jlspublishers.com or scan the QR code on the previous page.

ABOUT THE AUTHOR

Simon Rockwell writes from the ragged edge of failure and faith, where true change ignites. In 1994, a Caribbean accident claimed a pedestrian's life and shattered his world, hurling him into three decades of guilt's long shadow. That night could've ended it all. Instead, it cracked open the broken place where light seeps in.

Born two months premature in a small industrial town in Texas, Simon's story has always been one of improbable endurance. Two divorces schooled him in love's pitfalls. Shifts through Episcopal, LDS, and non-denominational circles revealed a God unbound by our tidy labels. Ventures built and buried across six continents hammered home the truth: no empire redeems what grace alone can heal.

Three years post-crash, in a Hong Kong coffee shop, Simon scrawled his rawest prayer on a tear-soaked napkin: "God, if you're still there after what I did..." That fragile scrap birthed God's Plan, Your Breakthrough.

Today, from his Texas home, Simon shares life with his wife, Stefaniya, whom he met at a Slavic Christian gathering in Hong Kong, their three kids, who dub Daddy's work "staring at screens and spilling his secrets," and who occasionally crash his 4 AM writing sessions with demands for 'emergency story time.'

From boardrooms to therapy couches, his resume boasts a business degree, decades in global consulting, sessions wrestling anxiety and PTSD, and midnight hotel-room grapples with the divine. But his deepest qualification: living proof that grace outlasts your gravest fall.

Simon's no guru who's nailed it. Last week: a Target meltdown. Yesterday: a frustrated snap at the kids, then a tearful make-up hug.

271

This morning: fresh doubts about Caribbean forgiveness. Yet here he stands, uncovering how your darkest hour might spark another's dawn.

For media queries, breakthrough tales, or your own napkin-prayer share, connect at www.jlspublishers.com.

www.ingramcontent.com/pod-product-compliance
Lightning Source LLC
Chambersburg PA
CBHW02121913O626
46554CB00004B/1286